Composition Concepts
for Band and Orchestra

Composition Concepts for Band and Orchestra

Incorporating Creativity in Ensemble Settings

Alexander Koops and John L. Whitener

Published in cooperation with the
National Association for Music Education

ROWMAN & LITTLEFIELD
Lanham • Boulder • New York • London

Published in cooperation with the National Association for Music Education
1806 Robert Fulton Drive, Reston, Virginia 20191
nafme.org

Published by Rowman & Littlefield
An imprint of The Rowman & Littlefield Publishing Group, Inc.
4501 Forbes Boulevard, Suite 200, Lanham, Maryland 20706
www.rowman.com

6 Tinworth Street, London SE11 5AL, United Kingdom

Copyright © 2020 by Alexander Koops and John L. Whitener

All rights reserved. No part of this book may be reproduced in any form or by any electronic or mechanical means, including information storage and retrieval systems, without written permission from the publisher, except by a reviewer who may quote passages in a review.

British Library Cataloguing in Publication Information Available

Library of Congress Cataloging-in-Publication Data

Names: Koops, Alexander, author. | Whitener, John L. author.
Title: Composition concepts for band and orchestra : incorporating creativity in ensemble settings / Alexander Koops and John L. Whitener.
Description: Lanham : Rowman & Littlefield Publishing Group, 2020. | Includes bibliographical references. | Summary: "This book is intended to introduce concepts about music composition to band and orchestra students of all ages"— Provided by publisher.
Identifiers: LCCN 2019051036 (print) | LCCN 2019051037 (ebook) | ISBN 9781475848908 (cloth) | ISBN 9781475848915 (paperback) | ISBN 9781475848922 (epub)
Subjects: LCSH: Composition (Music)—Instruction and study | Bands (Music)—Instruction and study. | Orchestra—Instruction and study.
Classification: LCC MT40 .K79 2020 (print) | LCC MT40 (ebook) | DDC 781.3071—dc23
LC record available at https://lccn.loc.gov/2019051036
LC ebook record available at https://lccn.loc.gov/2019051037

Contents

Foreword		vii
Acknowledgments		ix
Introduction		1
How to Use This Book		2
1	**Soundscapes**	5
	Teacher Guide: Lesson 1. Soundscapes	5
	Student Worksheet: Lesson 1. Soundscapes	8
	Teacher Guide: Lesson 1. Soundscapes: Supplemental Materials	10
2	**Timbre**	13
	Teacher Guide: Lesson 2. Timbre	13
	Student Worksheet: Lesson 2. Timbre	17
	Teacher Guide: Lesson 2. Timbre: Supplemental Materials	19
3	**Rhythm**	23
	Teacher Guide: Lesson 3. Rhythm	23
	Student Worksheet: Lesson 3. Rhythm	27
	Teacher Guide: Lesson 3. Rhythm: Supplemental Materials	29
	Test 1: Lessons 1–3. Soundscapes, Timbre, Rhythm	34
	Teacher Answer Key: Student Test 1. Lessons 1–3	36
4	**Melody**	39
	Teacher Guide: Lesson 4. Melody	39
	Student Worksheet: Lesson 4. Melody (Orchestra Version)	42
	Student Worksheet: Lesson 4. Melody (Band Version)	44
	Teacher Guide: Lesson 4. Melody: Supplementary Materials	46

5	**Ostinato**	51
	Teacher Guide: Lesson 5. Ostinato	51
	Student Worksheet: Lesson 5. Ostinato	55
	Teacher Guide: Lesson 5. Ostinato: Supplemental Materials	58
6	**Textures**	63
	Teacher Guide: Lesson 6. Textures	63
	Student Worksheet: Lesson 6. Textures	68
	Teacher Guide: Lesson 6. Textures: Supplemental Materials	72
	Test 2: Lessons 4–6. Melody, Ostinato, and Textures	76
	Teacher Answer Key: Test 2. Lesson 4–6	78
7	**Text-Based Composing**	81
	Teacher Guide: Lesson 7. Text-Based Composing	81
	Student Worksheet: Lesson 7. Text-Based Composing	86
	Student Worksheet: Lesson 7. Mozart's *Requiem: Dies Irae*—Listening	88
	Teacher Guide: Lesson 7. Text-Based Composing: Supplemental Materials	92
8	**Harmony**	99
	Teacher Guide: Lesson 8. Harmony	99
	Student Worksheet: Lesson 8. Harmony—Orchestra Version	105
	Student Worksheet: Lesson 8. Harmony—Band Version	110
	Teacher Guide: Lesson 8. Harmony: Supplemental Materials	114
9	**Form**	119
	Teacher Guide: Lesson 9. Form	119
	Student Worksheet: Lesson 9. Form	125
	Teacher Guide: Lesson 9. Form: Supplemental Materials	128
10	**Final Composition**	133
	Teacher Guide: Lesson 10. Final Composition	133
	Student Worksheet: Lesson 10. Final Composition Project	136
	Teacher Guide: Lesson 10. Final Composition: Supplemental Materials	139
	Test 3: Lessons 7–10. Text-Based Composing, Harmony, Form	143
	Teacher Answer Key: Test 3. Lessons 7–10	145

Appendix 1: Dynamics and Articulations Charts	149
Appendix 2: Glossary	151
Appendix 3: Sample Evaluation Form for Student Compositions	155
Appendix 4: Creative Warm-Ups for Band	157
Appendix 5: Recommended Resources	159
About the Authors	161

Foreword

One can think of many reasons why music educators tend to shy away from teaching composition or, at best, kick the can down the road, relegating it to a high school theory class. Some may feel they lack the skills or resources to teach it. Others worry that doing so could take away valuable time needed for rehearsals. Whatever the reasons, composition has always been a neglected child in school music programs. Even the most passionate advocates struggle with the dilemma of how and to what degree it should be taught in a band and orchestra setting.

Composition Concepts for Band and Orchestra by Alexander Koops and John L. Whitener is a new and exciting book that addresses this dilemma head on. Using this book, directors will be able to incorporate composition into their rehearsal settings in simple, meaningful ways, shining new light on what it means to be a musician. Students will be led on a journey of discovery through a series of 10 imaginative lessons, beautifully sequenced, each lesson building carefully upon its predecessor. Lessons are concise, each taking approximately 20 to 25 minutes to complete. Repertoire lists are provided at the end of each lesson, reinforcing and contextualizing concepts just learned and underscoring the notion that listening to established works is one of the most important endeavors for anyone who aspires to compose.

Perhaps the most exciting thing about the book is its emphasis on unique soundscapes, color, tension and repose, and texture—aspects that are often neglected in a traditional high school theory class. Traditional rules of harmony and part writing are *not* the emphasis of this book, and that's a good thing. The authors, knowing that too many rules can hinder creativity, place greater emphasis on intuition, expressive intent, and beauty of sound. Non-traditional approaches to notation (e.g., graphs, drawings, verbal instructions, etc.) are given just as much legitimacy as traditional notation. All of this makes it possible for teachers with little or no background in composition to successfully teach the lessons.

Composition Concepts for Band and Orchestra promises to be an important and valuable contribution to music education. Music teachers incorporating this book into their classes and rehearsals will foster in their students new ways of thinking, fire their imaginations, and empower them with the ability to *compose* their own music rather than simply perform compositions by others.

Frank Ticheli, Composer
Professor of Composition
Thornton School of Music
University of Southern California

Acknowledgments

The authors are indebted to many friends, family, colleagues, and students who have made this book possible.

Robert Cutietta—Dean, Thornton School of Music, University of Southern California. For encouragement, wisdom, and support and launching John's career in higher education.

Morten Lauridsen—Composition professor, Thornton School of Music, University of Southern California. For his creative wisdom and inspiration teaching John and contributing so fully to the art, profound beauty, and craft of music.

Frank Ticheli—Composition professor, Thornton School of Music, University of Southern California. For writing the foreword, for serving on Xander's dissertation committee, and for offering composition lesson ideas for beginning composition. Also, for the amazing composition lessons for John and the friendship and fellowship we enjoy as colleagues and collaborators.

Peter Webster—Vice Dean, Thornton School of Music, University of Southern California. For offering a window into creativity for John from an incredible scholar, supportive colleague, and wonderful human being.

Families—Orhon Whitener, for her steadfast love and faith in her husband and for her constant support and encouragement for this project. Noni Bayarjavhlan, for the art and graphics titles, and Mimi Bayarjavhlan, for her joy and enthusiasm and positive, loving spirit. Shaelyn Theule-Koops, for her love, and Dana and Daniel Koops, for their creativity and encouragement.

To our students, past and present—for the privilege to both teach and learn from you.

Teacher Action Research team of middle school band directors: Jeff Grable, Eric Kooi, Ed Schoendorf, Karen Klagis, and Scott Taylor—for being willing to test out all the lessons and offer invaluable feedback.

Maude Hickey, Clint Randles, Alex Shapiro, David Stringham, and Linda Thornton—whom Xander was blessed to work with on *Musicianship: Composing in Band and Orchestra*, and who have each contributed to the greater work of developing composition teaching resources through books, articles, and conference sessions.

Introduction

> Creativity and innovation are essential for the development of the necessary skills to flourish in the 21st century, as well as to promote essential skills for successful student and workplace achievement.[1]

This book is intended to introduce concepts about music composition to band and orchestra students of all ages and engage them in actual creative, composing projects. The *National Core Arts Standards* (2014) emphasize that students should be engaged in the "creative practices of imagination, investigation, construction, and reflection in multiple contexts."[2] These lesson plans attempt to accomplish that challenge in the context of large group band and orchestra ensemble classes using composition activities and projects.

Leaders in the field of music education encourage composition because it allows students to express themselves in a personal way that is different from performing or listening to music. In both Western and non-Western cultures, music composition has been considered a musical activity equally as important as performance, improvisation, and analysis. The benefits of composition are many, including the development of musicianship skills, listening aptitude, and an understanding of contemporary music and music theory, as well as providing training for the beginning composer. Composing music offers a creative outlet for all music students.

Although many would agree that being involved with the process of music composition could be important for young music students, most public school music teachers shy away from including this field of study in their classrooms because of a lack of time, training, and/or performance pressure.[3] To address these problems, the composition lessons presented here have been specifically created to overcome the main roadblocks teachers face when teaching students to compose. For instance, all the lessons may be accomplished in a relatively short amount of time (20 to 25 minutes) during a regular instrumental ensemble rehearsal. The lessons are clearly and simply presented so that any music teacher can successfully teach them, regardless of whether they have a background in composition. Although the lessons may be taught in as little as 20 minutes, teachers have the option of extending their instruction longer as time permits, which is strongly recommended. Addressing the issue of performance pressure, our field experience has shown us that the quality of concerts, festivals and other performance requirements do not suffer as a result of teaching these lessons. Of course, teachers may consider arranging rehearsals and concerts with one or two easier pieces, or perhaps fewer pieces, in order to provide more classroom time for teaching these music composition concept lessons.

Another issue with most school ensemble settings is that students working individually or in small groups struggle to hear themselves amid the noise and chaos of everyone trying out compositional ideas in the same room. These lessons have been created so that the entire ensemble can work together creating compositions as one large group, rather than as individuals. If facilities are available and conducive to having individuals or small groups work on composition ideas during the class time, this is certainly an option. The emphasis here, however, is on group activities. Teachers should always feel free to encourage their students to compose music on an individual basis outside of class (such as for extra credit). It is the authors' sincere and fervent wish that these lessons will lead to a deep understanding and appreciation of the compositional process for music students and music teachers alike.

HOW TO USE THIS BOOK

The lessons here have been designed with an "elements of music" approach, covering the concepts of soundscapes, melody, rhythm, harmony, texture, timbre, and form. The lessons and activities have been placed in a specific order based on what worked best for teachers during the field-testing process, though teachers should always feel free to combine, adapt, or change the lessons to make them fit their own situations. The concepts of *tension and repose* (or *release*) and *unity and variety* are overarching ideas that may be emphasized in rehearsals of both the ensemble music and student compositions, as well as any work of art, for that matter. Lessons may always be supplemented with basic musical concepts such as meter, pitch, dynamics, having students conduct, or other interactive activities the director desires. *It is important that all students be engaged and actively compose and create as individuals and as a group as much as possible during every lesson.*

Whenever possible, teachers should attempt to connect the lessons to actual music the students are performing in class to help deepen their learning experience and add a practical component to the lesson. *Hopefully every lesson will always be connected in some way to the regular ensemble repertoire.* Teachers should also try to include the listening examples listed, or pick examples from their own personal collections of music. Students need to hear and perform diverse selections of music as part of their education in composition, as well as for their general musicianship and music education. Extra credit could be offered to students for bringing in short examples of music representing the concepts being taught to make the work relevant to the student. Including a variety of styles of music, such as using pieces from other cultures, should be encouraged and nurtured. Asking students to find and share a piece from their own cultural heritage that illustrates one of the composition concepts presented creates deep learning opportunities for all students and teachers.

Always solicit ideas from your students. Encourage them to come up with their own sounds and stories for the music. Students may be shy and reluctant at first, but our field experiences have shown that students very quickly become enthusiastic and excited about creating unique and interesting sounds that are then combined and organized in compositions. Make the lessons as student centered as possible, tapping into their natural curiosity and creativity. Let them explore and create. Be the "guide on the side" and assist their efforts.

Each lesson contains a teacher guide, a student worksheet, and a teacher supplementary section. At the beginning of each lesson, vocabulary words are listed. Certain words are in *italics* in the teacher version of the lesson, and left as a blank (_____) on the student worksheet. It is intended that students will fill in the blanks on their student worksheet as the teacher presents the lesson and the vocabulary.

Three tests are provided to help students review the material. Test 1 covers lessons 1–3, test 2 covers 4–6, and test 3 covers 7–10. At the end of the book, an optional music composition assessment rubric is provided, as well as a glossary and dynamics chart. All student worksheets may be photocopied as needed.

NOTES

1. *National Core Arts Standards: A Conceptual Framework for Arts Learning*, 2014, www.nationalartsstandards.org, 20, http://www.nationalartsstandards.org/sites/default/files/NCCAS%20%20Conceptual%20Framework_0.pdf.

2. *National Core Arts Standards*, 19.

3. A. Koops, *Incorporating Composition in Middle School Band Rehearsals* (DMA diss., University of Southern California, 2009).

Chapter One

Soundscapes

> Music is organized sound, but the organization has to involve some element of the unexpected or it is emotionally flat and robotic. . . . Composers imbue music with emotion by knowing what our expectations are and then very deliberately controlling when those expectations will be met, and when they won't. The thrills, chills, and tears we experience from music are the result of having our expectations artfully manipulated by a skilled composer and the musicians who interpret that music.
>
> —D. J. Levintin[1]

TEACHER GUIDE: LESSON 1. SOUNDSCAPES

> After completing this lesson, your students will be able to . . .
>
> Define *music, composing, composition,* and *soundscape.*
> Create and perform a soundscape composition involving at least four (4) different sounds.

Vocabulary Words

MUSIC: Music may be thought of as organized *sound and silence,* or more completely, music is sound and silence organized through time that communicates something to or has meaning for the listener.
COMPOSING: Composing involves *organizing* sound and silence in a manner that is designed and prepared in advance.

COMPOSITION: A musical composition is made up of sounds and silences that are organized by a person or (persons) in a purposefully *designed* way that can be consistently repeated.

SOUNDSCAPE: Just as a painter paints a *landscape*, a collection of natural scenery, or a *cityscape*, a picture of many buildings and shapes in a city, a composer might create a *soundscape*, which is a collection of conventional or unconventional sounds that are organized in some way.

Lesson Activities

See also Teacher Guide: Lesson 1. Soundscapes: Supplemental Materials at the end of the chapter for suggestions.

PLAY a piece from your current repertoire that has moments or passages of SILENCE.

DISCUSS how SILENCE occurs before, during, and after the musical piece that was played.

DEFINE music as "organized SOUND and SILENCE." Instruments make "expected" or "conventional" sounds. But music may use other, less expected or unconventional sounds too.

LISTEN to a musical piece that uses unconventional sounds and illustrates SOUNDSCAPE (e.g., "Avian Dance," "Whirlwind," "A Prehistoric Suite," "The Headless Horseman," etc.).

DISCUSS how music may use conventional sounds (e.g., from instruments or nature or electronics) or sounds that are used or combined in an unconventional way.

ILLUSTRATE the above concept by playing more music using SOUNDSCAPES (e.g., "Paper Cut," "Snakes!," "Follow the Drinking Gourd," etc.).

DISCUSS how sounds may be used to create a SOUNDSCAPE and organized into MUSIC.

CREATE a SOUNDSCAPE musical piece using unconventional sounds, such as:

Soundscape Composition 1

1. Say "Shhhhhhhhhhhhhhhh."	2. Silence.
3. Snap fingers.	4. Tap pencil on stand randomly—or all together on cue from the director.

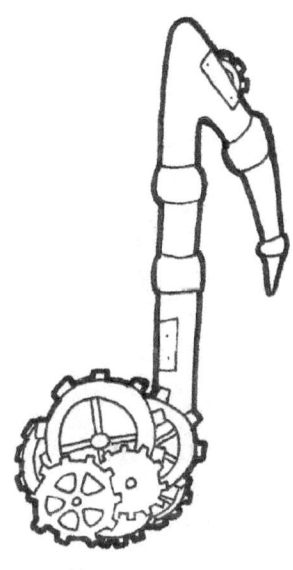

PRACTICE each sound or "part" individually, then combine two or more sounds at once. Use the suggested order or decide on a different one; use sounds individually or in combination.

PLAY your piece using the sounds together or separately, on cue from the director.

RECORD the piece, LISTEN and MODIFY it if you like, and RECORD again.

Using the STUDENT WORKSHEET, have students compose their own, unique soundscape.

REVIEW the concepts of MUSIC, SOUNSCAPE, COMPOSITION, and COMPOSING.

PERFORM the final group composition, and PLAY some student works as well.

STUDENT WORKSHEET: LESSON 1. SOUNDSCAPES

Name: _____ Date: _____

Vocabulary

Music: Music is _____ and _____ organized through time that communicates something to the listener or has meaning to the listener.

Composing: Composing involves _____ sound and silence in a manner that is designed and prepared in advance.

Composition: A musical composition is made up of sound and silence that is organized by a person or (persons) in a purposefully _____ way that can be repeated consistently.

Soundscape: Just as a painter paints a _____, a collection of natural scenery, or a _____, a picture of many buildings and shapes in a city, a composer might create a _____, which is a collection of conventional or unconventional sounds that are organized in some way.

Lesson Activities

Soundscape Composition 1

1. Say "Shhhhhhhhhhhhhhhh."	2. Silence.
3. Snap fingers.	4. Tap pencil on stand randomly—or all together on cue from the director.

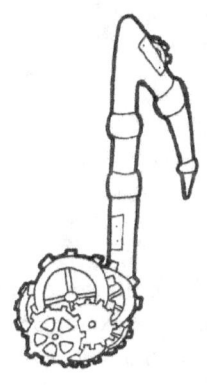

Write one idea of a unique sound you can make on your instrument or body:

With a friend(s), compose your own soundscape. Organize your ideas and sounds by filling in the box below.

Student Soundscape Composition

Sound 1
Sound 2
Sound 3
Sound 4

[Only this page authorized for duplication.]

TEACHER GUIDE: LESSON 1. SOUNDSCAPES: SUPPLEMENTAL MATERIALS

SOUNDSCAPES RECOMMENDED LISTENING

Recommended Composers	Sample Pieces
Benjamin Britten	*Four Sea Interludes*
John Cage	*Water Walk; In a Landscape*
Viet Cuong	*Re(new)al: Concerto for Percussion Quartet*
Edvard Grieg	"Morning" from *Peer Gynt*, op. 23
Ferde Grofé	"Sunrise" from *Grand Canyon Suite*
Olivier Messiaen	*Des canyons aux étoiles*
Karlheinz Stockhausen	*Gruppen*
Iannis Xenakis	"Metastasis," "Terretektorh"

Connection to Published Repertoire

Beneath is a sample repertoire list featuring pieces that have aleatoric or soundscape elements. These pieces were chosen because they are exemplary examples from well-known, published composers. Pieces at each grade level (difficulty level) were chosen so that music teachers with bands and orchestras of varying musical performance ability could all select an appropriate piece of literature for the skill level of their ensemble.

SAMPLE REPERTOIRE WITH SOUNDSCAPES

BAND

Blackshaw, Jody	"Whirlwind" (Grade 1)
Bukvich, Daniel	"Dinosaurs" (Grade 2)
Broege, Timothy	"The Headless Horseman" (Grade 2) (measures 1–10)
Jennings, Paul	"A Prehistoric Suite" (Grade 2)
Shapiro, Alex	"Paper Cut" (Grade 2.5)
Carnahan, John	". . . And the Antelope Play" (Grade 3)
Colgrass, Michael	"Old Churches" (Grade 3)
Duffy, Thomas	"Snakes!" (Grade 3)
Viet Cuong	"Diamond Tide" (Grade 3)
Smith, R. W."	"In a Gentle Rain" (Grade 4)
Pennington, John	"Apollo" (Grade 4)
Whitacre, Eric	"Cloudburst" (Grade 4.5)
Duffy, Thomas	"Crystals" (Grade 4/5)

ORCHESTRA

Easy to Medium

Brown, Earle	"Modules 1 and 2"
Rands, Bernard	"Agenda"
Meyer, Richard	"Le Divin Enfant"
Meyer, Richard	"Ear-igami"
Adler, Samuel	"A Little Bit of . . , Space . . . Time"
Yamada, Keiko	"Amadare" (Aleatoric)
Balmages, Brian	"Creatures" (Aleatoric)
Cummings, Walter	"Water Reflections" (Soundscape)
Reznicow, Joshua	"Avian Dance" (Soundscape)
McBrien, Brendan	"Contraption" (Band or Orchestra versions)

Medium to Difficult

Punwar, Katherine	"Follow the Drinking Gourd"
Meyer, Richard	"Curse of the Rosin Eating Zombies from Outer Space"
Schafer, R. Murray	"Statement in Blue"
Erb, Donald	*Bakersfield Pieces*
Hovhaness, Alan	"Floating World"

Lesson Activities

1. Ask students to meet with the people directly on either side of them, in groups of three, and come up with one or more sounds they like and they can make, not using their instruments in a traditional way and not limited to their instruments.
2. Give them one minute to experiment. Then pick four or more ideas from the class and write them on the board.
3. Pick a student conductor to come up and lead the class in the "new" composition with sounds picked by the class.
4. Compose a soundscape that starts happy, then turns sad, and then ends happy again. (If you have a hard time coming up with sad sounds, consider adding moaning, either vocally or through an instrument; experiment with low sounds and low percussion).
5. Come up with a theme for the composition to help organize it—such as, "funny and scary movie scene music," "chase music," "flying music," "dance music," and so on.
6. Make a two-group composition, instead of just one part . . . or even make three parts. Add dynamics and other expressive elements (different articulations, tempos, etc.).

> Always, always: perform student compositions.

Advanced Soundscape Composition Suggestion

	Part 1 (A)	Part 2 (B)	Part 3 (A')
Group 1 (LEFT)	Say "Shhhhhhhhhhh." FORTE	Make unvoiced mouth sounds (tongue clicks, etc.).	Laugh until cued for END. Start Fortissimo and DESCRESCENDO
Group 2 (RIGHT)	Laugh until cued to stop. Start pianissimo; then CRESCENDO	Ch . . . ch . . . ch . . . ch . . . . (together, as conducted)	Snap fingers quietly but as fast as you can; at the same time say, "Shhhhhhh." DESCRESCENDO

GO THE EXTRA MILE

Ask students to either compose a new soundscape of their own or bring to class an audio example of a soundscape in music they have listened to. Involve as many students as possible in the creation of new and different sounds and combinations of sounds, creating and experimenting as they compose soundscapes together and individually.

NOTE

1. D. J. Levitin, *This Is Your Brain on Music: The Science of a Human Obsession* (New York: Dutton, 2006), 169.

Chapter Two

Timbre

He began to play it with a deliciously gooey, chocolate legato. The notes sounded like pieces of cake strung together by sticky strands of chocolate icing.

—Bruce Adolphe[1]

TEACHER GUIDE: LESSON 2. TIMBRE

> After completing this lesson, your student will be able to . . .
>
> Define *timbre, instrumentation,* and *range* (high- and low-pitch registers).
> Create and perform a composition that has varying timbre through the use of instrumentation and/or range.

Vocabulary Words

TIMBRE: Timbre describes the quality of a sound that makes it unique from other sounds, such as the difference in quality between a trumpet and a violin performing the exact same *pitch*. The phrase *tone color* is another way to refer to timbre.

ORCHESTRATION or INSTRUMENTATION: Composers and arrangers select specific instruments to play the musical parts of a piece of music—such as clarinets on the melody, tuba on the bass part, and horns on the harmony. Orchestration refers to the job the composer does when choosing *instruments* for the different musical parts of a piece of music.

RANGE: Quite simply, this refers to how *high in pitch* and how *low in pitch* an instrument can play. Think about your own voice. How low can you speak and how high can you "squeak"? This would be the range of your voice. Most instruments can produce low and high sounds.

Lesson Activities

See also Teacher Guide: Lesson 2. Timbre: Supplemental Materials at the end of the chapter for suggestions.

CHOOSE a piece or exercise that the band already performs where everyone can play the theme in unison (for example, an exercise from your method book or a scale, etc.).

PLAY the exercise or piece, and then have individual instrument sections play (e.g., all the flutes play, then all the trumpets play, then maybe clarinets and bells, and other combinations, including small combinations of only two or three performers as well as large groups, such as 20 performers, etc.).

ASK the questions, "What makes the flute sound different from the clarinets? Why do trumpets sound different from saxophones?"

TELL students, "There is a word we use to describe the difference in sound: TIMBRE."

NOTICE how some instruments have "low sounds" or "low pitches" (e.g., tuba, electric bass, bass clarinet, etc.) and some instruments are "higher" in pitch (e.g., flute, oboe, trumpet, etc.).

EXPLAIN and illustrate how COMPOSERS can select different instruments, having them play diverse musical ideas to create various combinations of sounds, or TIMBRES. A composer will select various TIMBRES for a musical composition just as an artist selects various COLORS for their painting.

DISCUSS how an important part of composing is choosing the TIMBRE, or sound, of each of your musical ideas. This is also referred to as ORCHESTRATION or INSTRUMENTATION.

COMBINE a VARIETY of sounds/colors/timbres using different instruments in several combinations (e.g., flutes and trumpets, clarinets and bells, trombones and saxophones, etc.) and have them play a simple passage, melody, or exercise.

LISTEN to the low and high RANGE of several instruments. High-pitched sounds on a clarinet have a different TIMBRE than very low-pitched sounds on a clarinet (e.g., have a clarinet play their low E and then an E in the mid-range). Have trombones play a low B-flat and a B-flat an octave higher; ask flutes to play low-pitched and high-pitched sounds, and so on.

EXPERIMENT with making sounds. Give students five minutes to play on their own and/or with a classmate on the same or different instrument, and come up with interesting TIMBRES or "colors" with traditional and/or nontraditional ways of playing their instruments. Suggestions might include the following: play on the mouthpieces only on any instrument; clarinet playing into timpani, trumpets/horns/euphoniums/tubas playing with valves pressed halfway, trombones playing without mouthpiece, trumpets playing in their low range with horns in their high range (or all brass on unison/octave pitches versus single brass on those pitches); flutes playing in unison with saxophones and other combinations of instruments; whistling, body sounds, clapping, tapping stands or water glasses, bowed vibes, PVC pipe, pots and pans, wood blocks, and so on.

PLAY some solo or small ensemble demonstrations of different colors (timbres).

Group Composition Suggested Starting Point: A BIG DOG Chasing a TINY BIRD

WRITE down ideas students have for what instrument or nontraditional ways of playing an instrument would be used to represent a big dog and a tiny bird, and also "chase music" ideas.

EXPERIMENT with individuals in class trying to represent "big dog," "tiny bird," or "chase" sounds on various instruments. For example, trombones may perform short, loud glissandos representing dog barks; percussion, for barks; flutes or piccolo, for bird sounds. See the supplementary materials at the end of the chapter for more ideas.

Each student should write down on a piece of paper what instruments (color or timbre) he or she thinks would represent each musical idea and whether the pitch range should be high, medium, or low. Then as a class vote on each one and write the description on the board.

DISCUSS a possible scenario for performing a piece of music about a big dog chasing a tiny bird. Will the dog be barking from the start or only after hearing or seeing the bird? How will you represent the chase? What is the order of events? How long will it last? How will it end?

PERFORM the composition and RECORD it.

LISTEN back to the recording. If there is time, consider revising and re-recording.

(Note: This lesson could naturally include a lot of discussion and artistic decision-making about rhythm, speed, articulation, and dynamics, which is fine! Encourage student ideas. Just make sure to isolate the concepts of *timbre* and *range* as important parts of the lesson.)

STUDENT WORKSHEET: LESSON 2. TIMBRE

Name: _____ Date: _____

Vocabulary

Timbre: Timbre describes the quality of a sound that makes it unique from other sounds, such as the difference in quality between a trumpet and a violin performing the exact same _____. The phrase "_____" is another way to refer to timbre.

Orchestration or instrumentation: Composers and arrangers select specific instruments to play the musical parts of a piece of music, such as clarinets on the melody, tuba on the bass part, and horns on the harmony. Orchestration refers to the job the composer does when choosing _____ for the different musical parts of a piece of music.

Range: Quite simply, this refers to how _____ and how _____ an instrument can play.

Lesson Activities

Come up with interesting *timbres* with traditional or nontraditional instruments (e.g., using your mouthpiece only, clicking the keys of your instrument, etc.). Be ready to demonstrate your idea to the class as a solo. *List your timbre exploration ideas here:*

Using the following idea and the tools you learned to build soundscapes from lesson 1, try to think of what TIMBRE (instrumental colors) would best represent your idea.

A Big Dog Chasing a Tiny Bird!

List the instrument(s) and how they could be used to portray this:

Big Dog: Pick which instrument/timbre (flute, oboe, clarinet, bassoon, saxophone, horn, trumpet, trombone, tuba, percussion, violin, viola, cello, bass, or others). List instrument(s) here:

Tiny Bird: Pick which instrument/timbre (flute, oboe, clarinet, bassoon, saxophone, horn, trumpet, trombone, tuba, percussion, violin, viola, cello, bass, or others). List instrument(s) here:

Chase music: Pick which instrument/timbre (flute, oboe, clarinet, bassoon, saxophone, horn, trumpet, trombone, tuba, percussion, violin, viola, cello, bass, or others), and describe how you would illustrate the "chase." List instrument(s) here:

Describe a composition using the above timbres:

[Only this page authorized for duplication.]

TEACHER GUIDE: LESSON 2. TIMBRE: SUPPLEMENTAL MATERIALS

Listening

RECOMMENDED LISTENING FOR TIMBRE

Ludwig van Beethoven	Symphony no. 6 "Pastoral": movement 4, "Storm and Tempest"
Ferde Grofé	"Sunrise" from Grand Canyon Suite
Edgard Varèse	"Intégrales"
Ludwig Göransson and Kendrick Lamar	*Black Panther* (movie soundtrack)
Avicii	"Levels"
Skream—Big Apple Records	"Promo Mix," January 2004

Connection to Published Repertoire

SAMPLE REPERTOIRE FOR TIMBRE

BAND

Blackshaw, Jody   "Belah Sun Woman" (Grades 1–2)

This is designed as a yearlong project piece for young band and has more complexity and challenge as the movements progress; it starts at grade 1 and progresses to grade 2 level. It is a fantastic piece to use to dialogue about timbre with young composers. In addition to the traditional band instruments, Blackshaw features chanting, snapping, stamping, *patsch*, pat chest, scrunch cellophane, pop bubble wrap, Joia tubes, rice rattle, claves, conga, bass guitar, string bass, solos, and features for woodwinds, brass, and percussion.

Jennings, Paul   "A Prehistoric Suite" (Grade 1+)

Throughout the whole suite, various instrument groups get featured with melodic lines, which is one important thing to point out to students on the topic of timbre. However, in the third movement, the band gets to have an improvisatory aleatoric section that really opens up the possibilities to discuss timbre and make decisions as an ensemble about what timbres to emphasize and why, as the ensemble is asked to re-create the sounds of a dinosaur battle!

Sweeny, Michael   "Ancient Voices" (Grade 2)

Creative use of singing and recorders in addition to traditional band instruments make this piece a great example of how a composer can use timbre to really make the concept of "ancient voices" come to life. Additional sound effects include tapping pencils on stands, blowing wind through the instruments, and key clicking. All of these are superb examples of the diverse timbres that a composer can draw out of the traditional concert band.

Broege, Timothy   "The Headless Horseman" (Grade 2)

There is mysterious and scary music at the beginning, followed by the sound of a horse galloping and a theme that matches the spirit of the story of the headless horseman. The orchestration choices are very creative, such as trombone glissandos in the low range. There are also a euphonium solo and a muted trumpet solo providing additional timbre choices not found in typical, young band repertoire.

Ticheli, Frank   *Simple Gifts*, Movement 1: "In Yonder Valley" (Grade 2+)

At the beginning of the movement, the flute plays and represents a bird singing. This movement is all about nature! Listen with a pastoral, "animals in nature" perspective, and have your students think about what timbres Ticheli chooses and why.

Mackey, John   "Foundry" (Grade 3)

Images of steel work are incorporated through sounds of percussionists hitting steel. Very mechanical band sounds are used that represent the title well!

Shapiro, Alex   "Paper Cut" (Grade 3)

This piece features an electronic sound track as well as a variety of sounds created by the performers using sheets of paper (i.e., crumple, snap, etc.), thus providing a rich exploration of timbres well beyond the traditional band instruments

ORCHESTRA

Bernofsky, Lauren   "Kalimba Lullaby" (Grade 1)

This all-pizzicato work for young strings imitates the kalimba, an African instrument also known as an mbira or thumb piano. This work allows you to discuss the special "timbre" of pizzicato, but also explore the sounds of the original African instruments as well, either through listening to YouTube examples, or bringing in actual kalimbas for students to try in class.

Day, Susan H.   "Eagle's Pride" (Grade 1.5)

This piece uses many special techniques (tremolos, double stops, and pizzicato) as well a variety of dynamics and therefore is a great way to introduce timbre in string orchestra.

Johnson II, Daryl   *Serenade and Fantasy for Strings* (Grade 2)

The *Serenade* contrasts pizzicato with arco, while the *Fantasy* uses a leitmotif that starts in the violas and expands to the other strings, providing a perfect introduction to an explanation of various timbres composers can use to bring out different feelings and moods.

Day, Susan   "Dragon Fire" (Grade 2+)

Imagine the fire-spewing, slimy-scaled mythical creature in this excellent teaching piece in A and E minor! Features many techniques including hooked bowings, slurs, lifts, accents, pizzicato, and tremolo. These are all important timbre-related concepts!

Punwar, Katherine   "Follow the Drinking Gourd" (Grade 3)
Composer Katherine Punwar uses col legno and pizzicato as well as other special effects in this creative setting of the traditional African American spiritual. Instructions include, "Tap shoulders or body of cello like a drum," and, "Wood of bow slides up and down string to create sound of light wind."

Adler, Samuel   "A Little Bit of . . . Space . . . Time" (Grade 4)
String instruments utilize their specific timbre capabilities to imaginatively capture feelings of being in space or, from an abstract, musical composition standpoint, the exploration of unique timbres in a string orchestra setting.

Lesson Activities

1. Big Dog, Little Bird, and Chase music ideas, which emphasize TIMBRE and RANGE:

   a. Big Dog—snare drum, woodblock, trumpets jumping forte, trombones "barking" by playing accented notes, or with glissandi that sound like barks (most likely LOW RANGE).
   b. Little Bird—violin, flute are natural choices, but encourage other creative ideas: brass produce whistle by blowing on shank end of mouthpiece, clarinets playing high screeches on mouthpiece, viola cello bowing above the bridge, and so on (most likely HIGH RANGE).
   c. Chase—saxophones, keyboard percussion instruments, and horns running up and down scales. Naturally this can be fast paced, very rhythmic, high energy, loud dynamics, screeches, mouthpieces, sound effects, and so on (probably LOW TO HIGH RANGE).

2. Pick a picture to show, imagine a geographical location, or have the students come up with a visual scene they want to represent musically. For example, ask the students where a place is that they would like to visit or go on vacation—maybe a beautiful beach: use marimba, suspended cymbal, flutes, and clarinets in long tones, in MEDIUM-TO-LOW RANGE. (The teacher can emphasize good tone and assign pitches, such as flutes on C and D, alternating—something simple but "colorful.") Small waves breaking could be represented by a suspended cymbal crescendo and then resting for a period of time, then repeating. Building on lesson 1 soundscapes, the ensemble members could verbally say "shhhhhhhhh" or blow wind through their instruments. If you want to add some "real" notes, have some whole note, descending scales, or fragments representing the sun setting.

3. Combine the above scenes into one large group composition—layered, or continuous, or developed.
4. Record and playback the composition(s); listen critically and revise the composition(s) to make it (them) better or different. Ask the students what they liked and didn't like as they listened to the recording. Consider trying different timbres (instrumentation). Record again.

GO THE EXTRA MILE

Ask students to compose, at home, a new piece of their own that explores at least two or more different timbres. Also encourage them to collaborate on a piece with a person who plays a different instrument so they can perform their composition showing off the different timbres of different instruments. Alternately, ask students to bring an audio example to class of a piece they have heard that has unique timbres.

NOTE

1. Bruce Adolphe, *What to Listen for in the World* (New York: Limelight Editions, 1996), 17.

Chapter Three

Rhythm

I got rhythm . . . Who could ask for anything more?

—Ira Gershwin

Combinations that have at their disposal twelve notes in each octave and all possible rhythmic varieties promise me riches that all the activity of human genius will never exhaust.

—Igor Stravinsky[1]

TEACHER GUIDE: LESSON 3. RHYTHM

After completing this lesson, your students will be able to . . .

Define *rhythm* and *pattern*.
Create and perform a musical composition based on a rhythm from life.
Explain in their composition how they have incorporated patterns.

Optional: Differentiate aurally and visually between free rhythm and strict rhythm with duple (2) or triple (3) meter.

Optional: Differentiate between simple meters and compound meters.

Vocabulary Words

PATTERN: A regular or repetitive form or a *repeated* design. Patterns are all around us.

BEAT: The steady, repetitive *pulse* or emphasis in music, like the human heartbeat.

METER: The organization or grouping of beats in music, such as *duple* (two beats per measure) or *triple* (three beats per measure).

SIMPLE METER: The beat is divisible by two (e.g., 2/4, 3/4, 4/4).

COMPOUND METER: The beat is divisible by three (e.g., 6/8, 9/8, 12/8).

RHYTHM: A *pattern* of beats/pulses in music.

FREE RHYTHM: A rhythm pattern that does *not* stay in any set pattern.

STRICT RHYTHM: A rhythm pattern that remains *steady*.

TEMPO: The *speed* of the main pulse of a piece of music.

Lesson Activities

See also Teacher Guide: Lesson 3. Rhythm: Supplemental Materials at the end of the chapter for suggestions.

PLAY a piece from your current repertoire that has moments or passages of strict rhythm and/or passages of free rhythm. Also consider taking a section of a piece in strict rhythm, but try playing it free rhythmically.

DISCUSS the feel of the meter in the musical piece, and note if it was duple or triple, simple or compound, free or strict. Be sure to emphasize the definition of meter as *the organization or grouping of beats in music, such as duple, triple, or compound meter*. Define rhythm as a *pattern of beats* in music. Help students discover the difference between rhythm and meter.

ILLUSTRATE the beat or pulse in music. Have students clap the pulse in a few of the pieces you play. Point out how beats are commonly grouped together (meter) in groups of two, three, or four.

SING "Row, Row, Row Your Boat" and figure out if it is duple or triple meter. Then sing "Happy Birthday" and do the same. Try this with "Mary Had a Little Lamb" or "Ode to Joy."

LISTEN to an excerpt of a musical piece and identify the meter and rhythmic patterns.

DISCUSS the feel of the meter in the music, and note if it was duple or triple, or simple compound, free, or strict.

Rhythm

EXPLAIN that composers all use rhythm as a basic building block of composition.

DISCUSS what feelings a composer might try to express using a fast tempo (excitement, joy, terror). How about a slow tempo (reflective, sadness, love)?

EXPLORE by looking for patterns in life—both aural and visual. If needed, begin by pointing out examples such as ceiling tiles, windows, rows of desks, cell phone ringtones, and so on. Note the pulse of the patterns or the natural rhythm included in the examples. Especially note if the visual patterns come in duple or triple groupings. How they are organized? (Can you relate that to the music you know?)

ASK students if the sounds of a train would be strict or free, and compare that to the sounds of a bee buzzing around or a bird singing. Consider connecting the conversation to music repertoire such as Steve Reich's "Different Trains" or Rimsky-Korsakov's "Flight of the Bumble Bee." Look for patterns in nature that express themselves in music.

EXPLAIN that in music, patterns help organize and give a framework for the mind to understand and enjoy what is being heard. We are programmed to try and hear patterns, repetitions, imitations, and variations. Connect to the vocabulary for this chapter and explain that a pattern is a regular or repetitive form or a *repeated* design. Beat, pulse, and rhythm all occur in patterns.

IMAGINE patterns of sounds that create rhythm in our lives![2] Take a walk with me. . . . We wake up in the morning:

1. Listen to our alarm clock: "Beep, beep, beep." (strict or free?)
2. Then we brush our teeth: "Scrub, scrub, scrub—spit." (strict or free?)
3. In the kitchen we hear slurp, slurp, slurp of our little brother eating cereal and mom and dad drinking coffee or tea. (strict or free?)
4. At school, we hear the bell ring every 49 minutes, signaling the change of classes. (strict or free?)
5. Ocean waves roll in one after another, building and crashing. (strict or free?)

Have students DESCRIBE and write down ONE rhythm from life—either visual OR aural—on their student handout. Try to get the students to DESCRIBE or NOTATE the rhythm and make sure it can be extended as a pattern. For example, if the rhythm is a pattern of windows, they could draw a whole line of windows. If the pattern is a clock ticking, they should write out the ticking for a whole line. If they are unsure of how to describe it or notate it, the teacher can help.

DISCUSS if instruments, voices, or soundscapes could be created to represent any of these life rhythms in some way for a musical composition.

WRITE some of the students' ideas on the board. VOTE on which ideas/rhythms might be adaptable to a group musical composition.

PICK one idea and compose a group composition. Use soundscapes, different timbres, and patterns of rhythms incorporating what has been learned in previous lessons.

PRACTICE the composition. Notice the patterns in the piece and the order of sounds.

Consider LAYERING rhythms on top of one another.

RECORD the piece, LISTEN and MODIFY if you like, and RECORD again.

Sample Composition Idea

Train coming and going: Build on the previous lessons. How do we make a sound that sounds like a train coming down the tracks? What timbre? Train soundscape?

1. In a band, have the snare drum start *pp* and do a regular repeated pattern of eighth notes: every four snare hits, then the bass drum plays. With strings, begin with violins col legno and then add in the rest of the orchestra. Make it rhythmic and repeated.
2. Slowly the whole ensemble joins in the rhythm and crescendos to *fff*. In a concert band, all the woodwinds could take off their mouthpieces and give "twooo, twoooo" representing the train's locomotive whistle blowing. In a string orchestra, the violins could try to create a sound that imitates the whistle of a train ("Orange Blossom Special" fiddle tune, etc.).
3. Fade away, decrescendo to just a few instruments, fade out.
4. Is this duple or triple? Could you choose to make it either? A nice rhythm can be created in 4/4. Have beat one be the strongest accent; beat two, weak; three, somewhat strong; four, the weakest. This really emphasizes the way 4/4 time should traditionally be played (great connection to "regular" music)!

STUDENT WORKSHEET: LESSON 3. RHYTHM

Name: _____ Date: _____

Vocabulary

Pattern: A regular or repetitive form or a _____ design.

Meter: The organization or grouping of beats in music, such as _____ meter or a triple meter.

Beat: The steady, repetitive _____ or emphasis in music, like the human heartbeat.

Rhythm: A _____ of beats in music.

Free rhythm: A rhythm pattern that does _____ stay in any set pattern.

Strict rhythm: A rhythm pattern that remains _____.

Tempo: The _____ of the main pulse of a piece of music.

Lesson Activities

Rhythm from life: *Write down or describe* a rhythm from life. Either write the rhythm or draw the pattern somehow and describe how you would get your rhythm from life to be performed by an individual or ensemble. (Option: see if your pattern is a more duple or triple feeling, and label it with phrase markings or bar lines. Ask your teacher for help if needed).

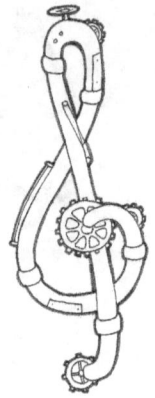

Step 1: Write or describe the rhythm here:

OPTIONAL Step 2: Add pitch according to your teacher's directions (low, medium, high, or specific pitches), or write down the group composition.

[Only this page authorized for duplication.]

TEACHER GUIDE: LESSON 3.
RHYTHM: SUPPLEMENTAL MATERIALS

Listening

RECOMMENDED LISTENING FOR RHYTHM

Steve Reich   *Different Trains*
This music uses actual human speech that is recorded and incorporates it into the texture of a string quartet, representing train rides at different times in history and in different places all over the world.

Karel Husa   *Music for Prague 1968*
The final movement has a "Morse code" kind of rhythm, representing a distress call. This music was written at the time the Russians were invading Prague.

Gustav Holst   "Hammersmith"
The introductory music, repeated as a base ostinato motive, represents the River Thames, and then a bird call comes in.

Rimsky-Korsakov   "Flight of the Bumble Bee"
This fun music speaks for itself!

Percy Grainger   *Lincolnshire Posy*, Movement 5, "Lord Melbourne"
Creative use of free rhythm representing a swaggering and boastful soldier singing about his great victories, though now he is on his deathbed.

Connection to Published Repertoire

SAMPLE REPERTOIRE FOR RHYTHM

BAND

Loest, Timothy "Traffic Jam" (Grade 1)

This light rock number includes a groovin' percussion part and lots of car horn noises and creative use of rhythms to inspire students to create new compositions with fun rhythm.

Broege, Timothy *Train Heading West and Other Outdoor Scenes* (Grade 2)

Each of the movements—Prairie Ritual, Rain on the Mountains, and Train Heading West—has a unique, descriptive character with interesting compositional techniques to create the mood. Great examples of rhythm!

Balmages, Brian "Rhythms and Riffs" (Grades 2–3)

As the title suggests, various grooves and riffs are built into the ensemble throughout as the piece develops harmonically, melodically, and rhythmically.

Peck, Russell. "Cave (Cave of the Winds)" (Grade 4)

Starts with a heartbeat imitation in the bass drum, then develops in a fun groove, with some jazz influence. Great use of a rhythm from a "heartbeat" being developed.

ORCHESTRA

Dackow, Sandra (arr.). "Burgundian Carol," traditional French carol, attributed to Bernard de la Monnoye (Grade 1)

There are optional percussion parts that your string players can cover; though not essential, adding any of the percussion parts greatly enhances the performance and is a great way to discuss composing rhythm and how much it can add to a composition.

Meyer, Richard "Bio Rhythms" (Grade 2)

Uses body percussion—a great way to introduce creative composition ideas related to rhythm.

Sharp, Thom "Lost Horizon" (Grade 2.5)

This energetic, adventure-themed rondo has every section taking the lead and heading off into the horizon looking for adventure. The rhythm of the main theme is used for new melodies in the contrasting sections, either in its original form or starting on a different beat to create a new, yet familiar, rhythm. The last iteration of the main melody employs augmentation. All of these devices provide ample opportunity for instructing students about the importance of rhythm in form and structure.

Fagan, Gary	"Primal Strings" (Grade 3)

This is a great piece to challenge young players who are learning fundamental basics of rhythm and changing meters and to give interesting ideas for young composers to consider using creative rhythms.

Lesson Activities

For the "Train" student composition: Start with a soundscape representing a train starting up, and then work in a railroad melody like "I've Been Working on the Railroad" or "This Train Is Bound for Glory." Short quotations, sections, or hints of the original tunes are fine—no need for an exact full quote of the original!

Help the students connect the concepts of a train and tracks to music. The railroad tracks have a pattern of wooden railroad ties, interspersed by huge nails that hold the ties in place (like measures in music). Then every ten railroad ties, there is a new piece of steel railroad (like phrases in music). The tracks are interspersed with road crossings, bridges signs, and railway stations (like sections of a piece of music)!

Additionally, each train that follows the tracks has a pattern: the engine, the cars, many of which are the same, but vary according to style and color—such as passenger cars, freight cars, semi-trailer cars, and so on, and possibly even a caboose or another engine or two at the end. Note: The train also creates an aural pattern as we listen to it go by us on the tracks! In addition to the steady, pulsing rhythms, we hear a crescendo and diminuendo with punctuations of loud whistles as the train approaches and passes.

Additional Patterns to Consider for Compositions

1. The pattern of windows in a building—some small, some big, all in a row up and down.
2. The pattern of instrument lockers or lockers in a gym or hallway at school.
3. The pattern of street lights, stop signs, trees along the edge of a street, mailboxes (regularly placed, but each might be unique in size and shape), parking meters, and so on.
4. The pattern of your fingerprints.
5. The pattern of leaves on a tree, petals on a flower, legs on a crawling bug.
6. The layers of different rock you can see as you descend down into the Grand Canyon.
7. The alternating sizes and colors of the planets of our solar system in outer space.
8. A double rainbow stretching across the sky after a rainstorm.

Concepts for Developing a Rhythmic Composition

Consider composing a rhythmic piece using only one pitch. Use different timbres, articulation, rhythms, articulations, tempos, and dynamics to make it interesting. Develop the piece by having the whole ensemble perform a given rhythm pattern twice; then feature a soloist or two, one or two times, then everyone one time again. It is a good individual compositional assignment to write a rhythmic piece all based on one pitch. For an advanced option, consider changing pitches to experiment melodically within a rhythm pattern, but limit the pitches to just two or three designated pitches, such as the first three pitches of the minor scale.

Try a short pattern in canon (e.g., pattern of 10 railroad ties—one group starts, after three counts a second group starts, etc.); add some varied rhythms such as dotted quarter or eighth rhythms; then do it twice as fast, half-time, and so on. Pick different meters—duple, triple, mixed. Conform composition rhythms to this meter pattern.

Sample School Day Soundscape

To build on the previous lesson on timbre, try the following "School Day Soundscape": the pattern of class periods in a school day, interrupted every 49 minutes by a bell. Represent this with a chosen soundscape interrupted by something representing the school bell and then returning to the chosen soundscape, or for a longer composition, a new soundscape representing a different class.

School Day Soundscape A: Everyone tapping on stand or instrument—representing typing on computers (writing a story for English class) or math class—percussionists on the rim of the drums or strings col legno. (Optional: try to do some triple or duple rhythmic feel.)

School Bell signaling switching class: Percussionist hits the chimes three times, or snare gives a loud roll or fast roll on bells and xylophone, and so on. (Optional: try to do some triple or duple rhythmic feel.)

School Day Soundscape B: Lots of short, fast, staccato sounds on instruments representing ball bouncing in PE class . . . swishes representing a basketball going through the hoop, and so on.

School Bell: Percussionists again.

School Day Soundscape C: Lunch time in the cafeteria . . . random clanking, laughing, belching, talking, slurping, noodling on instruments. (Can random be part of music? Yes!)

School Bell: Percussionists again.

School Day Soundscape D: Band or orchestra period—play a short snippet of one of your most fun or best loved *band or orchestra pieces*. (Optional: identify duple or triple feel.)
School Bell: Percussionists again, and so on.
End: Everyone shouts YEAH!!

Sample Computer Typing Music Composition

Fingers tapping on keypad of computer: Represent with snare drum with snare off or strings tap on their instruments or have the ensemble members tap on their stands. Vote on what the pattern should be. For example, three letter words are easy to type. Try to organize a composition that represents typing, with 3/4 meter, interspersed with rests as the person starts and stops typing words. The teacher could even prepare students for this to save some time by writing a pattern of quarter notes on the student handout. Then students could vote on having solos, alternating with everyone in the ensemble. By focusing only on one pitch, or allowing three to five pitches, but not more, the students can maintain the emphasis on rhythm and understanding rhythmic tools and developments.

Sample Alarm Clock Composition

Beep beep beep; hit snooze. Shhhhh, snore . . . , shhhh, snore. . . . Beep beep beep beep, repeat ad nauseum, then jump out of bed, "Ah, I'm late for school!!!!"

Sample Coffee Composition

Coffee grinder (kind of like a race car revving its engine): Trombone glissandos or celli/bass low glissandi. . . . Rotate grind/rev sound around the ensemble. Then pouring water sound, then boiling, dripping, pouring into mug . . . , and, at last, sipping delicious coffee and eating a pastry.

GO THE EXTRA MILE

Ask students to individually compose at home a new piece of their own that explores rhythms from life. Also encourage them to collaborate on a piece with a person who plays a different instrument. Alternately, ask students to bring an audio example to class of a piece they have heard that has unique rhythms or is inspired by a rhythm from life. Open up the options of composing the piece on Soundtrap® or Noteflight or other digital programs.

TEST 1: LESSONS 1–3. SOUNDSCAPES, TIMBRE, RHYTHM

Name: _____ Date: _____

Test 1 Questions 1 to 10

Match the following words with their correct definition by writing the correct letter in the blank:

1. _____ Music
2. _____ Strict rhythm
3. _____ Composing
4. _____ Instrumentation
5. _____ Duple rhythm
6. _____ Pattern
7. _____ Free rhythm
8. _____ Timbre
9. _____ Triple rhythm

A. A rhythm pattern that remains steady
B. Feeling or grouping of two beats
C. Composers and arrangers select specific instruments to play the musical parts of a piece of music, such as clarinets or violas on the melody
D. A regular or repetitive form or a repeated design
E. Sound and silence organized through time that says something to the listener or has meaning to the listener
F. The quality of a sound that makes it unique from other sounds, such as the difference in quality between a trumpet sound and a violin sound performing the exact same pitch
G. A feeling or grouping of three beats
H. A rhythm pattern that does not stay in any set pattern
I. The act of organizing sound and silence in a manner that is designed and prepared in advance

10. Relating to lesson 1, briefly write down a four-part soundscape, using sounds and silence as discussed in class by filling out the chart below.

Part 1	Part 2	Part 3	Part 4

11. Relating to lesson 2 "Timbre/Instrumentation," explain what instrument(s) you picked and how the instrument should play to represent the idea of a little, tiny bird.

[Only this page authorized for duplication.]

12. Describe a visual pattern or a rhythmic sound pattern you have seen or heard around you. Show and explain how that pattern might translate into music. (Use a separate sheet of staff paper if necessary.)

[Only this page authorized for duplication.]

TEACHER ANSWER KEY: STUDENT TEST 1. LESSONS 1–3

Test 1 Answers 1 to 10

Match the following words with their correct definition by writing the correct letter in the blank:

1. E   Music
2. A   Strict rhythm
3. I   Composing
4. C   Instrumentation
5. B   Duple rhythm
6. D   Pattern
7. H   Free rhythm
8. F   Timbre
9. G   Triple rhythm

A. A rhythm pattern that remains steady
B. Feeling or grouping of two beats
C. Composers and arrangers select specific instruments to play the musical parts of a piece of music, such as clarinets or violas on the melody
D. A regular or repetitive form or a repeated design
E. Sound and silence organized through time that says something to the listener or has meaning to the listener
F. The quality of a sound that makes it unique from other sounds, such as the difference in quality between a trumpet sound and a violin sound performing the exact same pitch
G. A feeling or grouping of three beats
H. A rhythm pattern that does not stay in any set pattern
I. The act of organizing sound and silence in a manner that is designed and prepared in advance

10. Relating to lesson 1, briefly write down a four-part soundscape, using sounds and silence as discussed in class by filling out the chart below.

Sample Composition

Part 1	Part 2	Part 3	Part 4
SAY "SHHHHHH"	SNAP	LAUGH OUT	CLAP ON CUE

11. Relating to lesson 2 "Timbre/Instrumentation," explain what instrument(s) you picked and how the instrument should play to represent the idea of a little, tiny bird.

Sample answer: I PICKED FLUTE PLAYING HIGH. I THINK A TINY BIRD WOULD HAVE A HIGH-PITCHED SOUND.

12. Describe a visual pattern or a rhythmic sound pattern you have seen or heard around you. Show and explain how that pattern might translate into music. (Use a separate sheet of staff paper if necessary).

Sample answer: TRAIN, OCEAN WAVES, STOPLIGHTS, WINDOWS, AND SO ON.

NOTES

1. Igor Stravinsky, *Poetics of Music in the Form of Six Lessons*, trans. Arthur Knodel and Ingolf Dahl (Cambridge, MA: Harvard University Press, 1947), 64, https://monoskop.org/images/6/64/Stravinsky_Igor_Poetics_of_Music_in_the_Form_of_Six_Lessons.pdf.
2. See also STOMP, www.stomponline.com. "The Exploration of Rhythm in Everyday Things," in *Stomp: A Study Guide*, Stomponline, 7, https://stomponline.com/stomp/pdf/study_guide.pdf.

* Only this page authorized for duplication © 2019 by Alexander Koops and John L. Whitener.

Chapter Four

Melody

There's a melody in everything. And once you find the melody, then you connect immediately with the heart. Because sometimes English or Spanish, Swahili or any language gets in the way. But nothing penetrates the heart faster than the melody.

—Carlos Santana[1]

TEACHER GUIDE: LESSON 4. MELODY

After completing this lesson, students will be able to . . .

Define *melody* and *improvising*.
Create and perform a melodic composition.

Vocabulary Words

MELODY: A series of musical *tones* that are grouped together to make a single musical idea. A good melody has *unity* and *variety*. Simple melodies use mostly notes that move *stepwise* and end on the *tonic* or home base tone. It usually has some *repetition*.

IMPROVISING: Making up music on the spot without *planning* it out or writing it down.

Lesson Activities

See also Teacher Guide: Lesson 4. Melody: Supplemental Materials at the end of the chapter for suggestions.

PLAY a piece from your current repertoire that has a great melody, or select soloists to play excerpts of pieces that show off great melodies from your method book or elsewhere.

LISTEN to one or more famous melodies such as "Ode to Joy" or "Theme from the *New World Symphony*" or even "Twinkle, Twinkle, Little Star." Draw the shape (how it rises and falls) of the first phrase on the board. Have students note the shape of the melody and then, as they listen, draw the shape of each phrase on their student handout.

DEFINE *melody* as a series of musical TONES (sounds) that are grouped together to make a single musical idea. A good melody has both UNITY (things that are the same, or repeated) and VARIETY (things that are different).

DISCUSS one of your listening examples, such as "Ode to Joy," noting the STEPWISE motion, limited number of skips, ending on the TONIC, where REPETITION occurs, and how the melody has UNITY and VARIETY.

PERFORM the B-flat scale (band) or D major scale (orchestra) and sample melody (see the student handout or create and share your own teacher-composed melody based on a scale).

EXPLAIN that composers often use parts of scales to make up their melodies, just as authors will combine words in different ways to create stories or poems ("Twinkle, Twinkle" is a great example, with its descending scale motion).

DISCUSS improvisation. What is it? DEFINE *improvisation* as making up or creating music on the spot without *planning* it out or writing it down. EXPLAIN that composers sometimes start the composing process by improvising musical ideas.

MODEL a few one-measure or two-measure improvisation examples by singing or playing on an instrument, and have students perform back the examples by ear.

Sample with Solfège

Teacher: *do do re re mi re do*. Students respond by playing *do do re re mi re do*.

Sample with Numbers

Teacher introduces numbers that represent major scale degrees (instead of solfège):

1 1 2 2 3 2 1 (e.g., B-flat B-flat C C D C B-flat or D D E E F-sharp E D)

Students respond by playing scale degrees.

1 1 2 2 3 2 1 (e.g., B-flat B-flat C C D C B-flat or D D E E F-sharp E D)

IMPROVISE using the first three to five notes of the major scale. (Point out that Beethoven uses just five notes to create his famous "Ode to Joy" melody!)

Everyone can improvise at the same time and choose any rhythm they want. Encourage them to not play too loudly. This will sound like chaos, but it is worth it to get everyone participating! Alternately, students may improvise one at a time or two at a time, work in different corners and spaces in the room, or split up and go into practice rooms or outside.

If possible, listen to several students' melodies as solos, and then pick one student's melody idea and write it on the board for everyone to practice and play, or have everyone learn it by ear, and don't worry about notating it. When learning by ear, have the selected student composer play their own melody as a solo while everyone else hums along to internalize the notes.

PERFORM melodies as a soloist/composer as well as an entire ensemble.

RECORD the melody, LISTEN and MODIFY if you like, and RECORD again.

COMPOSE AND NOTATE: Using music staff paper, have students compose and notate their own, unique melody (teachers may need to help). Alternately if digital devices such as Chromebooks, iPads, or computers are available, students could notate their melodies with programs like Flat, Noteflight, or MuseScore.

REVIEW the concepts of MELODY, UNITY, VARIETY, and IMPROVISATION.

Challenge students to think about stepwise motion versus jumps, and also how much UNITY and VARIETY they have.

Optionally, COMBINE several student melodies that seem to go together into a longer composition. If time allows, create a rondo composition or add a soundscape introduction and conclusion.

PERFORM the final group composition.

STUDENT WORKSHEET: LESSON 4.
MELODY (ORCHESTRA VERSION)

Name: _____ Date: _____

Vocabulary

Melody: A series of musical _____ that are grouped together to make a single musical idea.

A good melody has _____ and _____. It is mostly _____ and ends on the _____ or home base tone. It usually has some _____.

Improvising: Making up music on the spot without _____ it out or writing it down.

Lesson Activities

On the back of this paper, draw the shape of the melody your teacher plays for you.

Orchestra: Use the first five notes of D major to improvise an original melody.

Violins:

[Only this page authorized for duplication.]

Melody 43

Violas:

Cello/Bass:

After you have improvised several ideas for a melody, try to write down your melody here, either with traditional notation or any type of graphic notation or word explanations or using a digital device. Ask your teacher for help if needed.

[Only this page authorized for duplication.]

STUDENT WORKSHEET:
LESSON 4. MELODY (BAND VERSION)

Name: _____ Date: _____

Vocabulary

Melody: A series of musical _____ that are grouped together to make a single musical idea.

A good melody has _____ and _____. It is mostly _____ and ends on the _____ or home base tone. It usually has some _____.

Improvising: Making up music on the spot without _____ it out or writing it down.

Lesson Activities

On the back of this paper, draw the shape of the melody your teacher plays for you.

Band: Use the first five notes of B-flat major to improvise an original melody.

Flutes, bells, xylophone (C instruments, treble clef):

Clarinets, trumpets, tenor saxophone, treble clef baritone (B-flat instruments):

Alto saxophone (E-flat instruments):

Horn (F instruments):

Trombone, baritone bass clef, tuba, electric bass (C instruments, bass clef)

After you have improvised several ideas for a melody, try to write down your melody here, either with traditional notation or any type of graphic notation or word explanations or using a digital device. Ask your teacher for help if needed.

TEACHER GUIDE: LESSON 4.
MELODY: SUPPLEMENTAL MATERIALS

MELODY RECOMMENDED LISTENING

Johann Sebastian Bach, *Sleepers Awake*; Wolfgang Amadeus Mozart, *Eine kleine Nacht Musik*; Giacomo Puccini, "Nessun Dorma" from *Turrandot*; Sergei Prokofiev, "Dance of the Knights"; James Horner, *Titanic*, "My Heart Will Go On," performed by Celine Dion. For contrast, consider also playing music examples without melody: Brian Balmages, "Reverberations"; world music samples including African drumming and Indonesian gamelan; and so on.

SAMPLE REPERTOIRE WITH MELODIES

Sample repertoire with melody abounds! Arrangements of Bach, Mozart, and Beethoven are certainly classics for all music students to know, but music by contemporary composers, pop/commercial music, movie music, and world music with creative melodies should all be included. Consider a medley from the movie *Lord of the Rings*, a Sousa march, or an African tune like "Siyahamba," and be sure to have your whole ensemble learn to sing and play the melody! Writing out a "lead sheet" and having it available in all clefs and transpositions is a great way to introduce any piece of music, but especially important when teaching about composing melodies.

BAND

For bands that can play Grade 3 music, consider studying and performing Haley Woodrow's *Melting Pot* (Grade 3). She uses a theme and variations approach with modes based on the F melodic minor scale (ascending). Three key signatures appear in the work to identify the root and, therefore, the mode. The two flats at the beginning indicate the tonic is B-flat, but it is a B-flat Lydian dominant scale, which is the fourth mode of the F melodic minor scale. The middle section has four flats to indicate the tonic of F, in the minor mode. During this section, both the ascending and descending forms of the F melodic minor scale are utilized. In the last section, no sharps / no flats in the key signature indicates C as the tonic, but note that the notes in the music contain the lowered sixth and lowered seventh scale degrees, which is the fifth mode of the F melodic minor scale. An exercise is included at the back of the music with these three modes, which you may find to be a good educational opportunity to teach about the melodic minor scale. To connect with composition, students could develop a short melody based on a given scale, like Lydian, and then vary the melody by trying it in other scale settings, like whole tone or Dorian, and so on.

ORCHESTRA

For orchestra, consider programming *Professor Wigstein's Amazing Melody Machine* by Richard Meyer (Grade 2.5). This fun and original piece for string orchestra introduces the technique of "tone painting." It depicts inventor Professor Wigstein's proud creation, a machine that plays some of the world's most famous melodies. The introduction portrays the ceremonious (and rather pompous) unveiling of the amazing machine. With four turns of its crank, the machine comes to life, grinding and churning as it prepares to produce a melody. "Ode to Joy" is heard, played pizzicato by the entire orchestra, and appropriately accompanied by generic "machine" sounds (ratchet and bell). Soon, the machine winds down, and the melody comes to a halt. Once again, the machine is cranked and begins working at another tune; *Eine kleine Nachtmusik* is heard. The machine winds down again, only to be cranked up a third time. The melody to Offenbach's "Can-Can" emerges. Midway through the tune, however, something goes wrong with the machine. Fragments of all three melodies are heard (in a variety of clashing keys) as the machine goes out of control, eventually exploding. A few hisses, and some dying moans are emitted. Finally, Chopin's "Funeral March" is heard as the machine plays its own death knell, dying with a final, soft hiss. To connect with composition lessons, any of these melodies could be developed as a theme and variations.

Lesson Activities

DISCUSS music with melody, music without melody, and where students have heard melodies. They may have heard them on the radio, online, from the TV, in the elevator, in the the mall, in music class, or in nature (birds). What styles of music have melodies (hip hop, pop, classical, folk, jazz)? Ask if there are styles or types of music that don't have melody (rap? soundscapes? minimalist?). To illustrate this, play examples of music without melody.

DISCUSS various ways to compose melodies and consider using a name or word to create a melody.

1. Frank Ticheli, "Postcard." Ticheli uses the letters from the name "ETHEL" to create his second theme.
2. Johann Sebastian Bach puts his name in various melodies. (See Wikipedia for examples.)

    BACH = B in German is B-flat in music notation; A; C; H—in German H is used for B-natural.

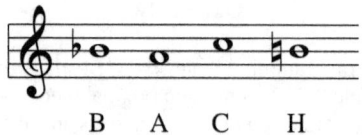

B A C H

One place Bach uses his "signature" name in music is in a fugue subject in the last Contrapunctus of *The Art of Fugue*.

3. Dmitri Shostakovich puts his name in his Symphony no. 10. (See Wikipedia for more details.) He abbreviates his name to DSCH to create a motif consisting of the musical notes D, E-flat, C, B-natural. In German musical notation, the E-flat is verbally pronounced or sung as "Es." D is for Dimitri, and the SCH is for his last name Shostakovich. In his Symphony no. 10, third movement, he uses this "signature."

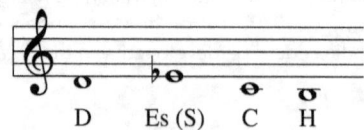

D   Es (S)   C   H

After listening to some examples, and ideally looking at a written music example of the above, have the students try to create a melody from a name or word. Use the letters A through G and see what names or words they can come up with and turn into music. Make sure to challenge them to give character to the melody using interesting rhythms, dynamics, and articulations.

DISCUSS what other ways composers build melodies.

Nature: Olivier Messiaen used bird songs to build a lot of his melodies.

Scales: Messiaen also used special scales (modes of limited transposition, whole tone scales, etc.). Composers often base their melodies on a certain scale, such as a B-flat major scale, or G-minor scale. Asian music is often built using the pentatonic scale, and "the blues" has its own scale. Each scale creates a different flavor or feeling to the music.

Words imitated in music—for example, in *Different Trains* by Steve Reich: Actual words are put into a recorded electronic sound track that is mixed with a live string quartet. The string instruments copy the exact pitch and inflection of the spoken words from interviews done with people riding trains in the 1940s in Europe and America (also see chapter 5 on ostinato to build on this concept).

COMPOSE: Write a given rhythm on the board. Students improvise with that rhythm using the pitches of a selected pentatonic scale. A one-measure rhythm of any kind, repeated, works well, such as quarter-quarter-half, or something more complex, appropriate to the level of the ensemble.

CALL AND RESPONSE: "I'll play one measure, then you try to copy me." Have some volunteers do solos, and the whole ensemble can either try to copy them or plays a standard response that the teacher suggests or class votes on.

IMPROVISATION: Try some call and response, where the answer phrase is slightly changed.

COMPOSE: Write down on the board one or two melodies composed by students in the class and have everyone practice the melody or melodies together. (Either transpose them quickly on the board for all instruments, use numbers or solfège to signify the scale degrees, or simply teach the melodies by rote. Also consider having your digital device handy and quickly inputting the solo into a notation program such as Noteflight or Notion in a prepared, full-ensemble score, and then quickly copy and paste the melody into all the other instruments so the ensemble can immediately read it as a class.) Alternate newly composed solos with the full ensemble playing the melody on the board.

RECORD the melody improvisation and composition process as it happens in class with solo ideas being contributed by ear. Do not worry about writing them down, but after class, use the recording to notate the melodies and share them in a transposed version for every instrument in the following class period.

REVIEW the opening activity where students drew the curve/shape of the melody: Often it is nice to have a melody that goes in an arching phrase, building up to a high note and then going back down at the end. Look for one of these or create one.

REFLECT: Ask the students what creates *unity* to the feeling of a melody? In a musical question and answer, the rhythm can be a great unifier, even if the pitches are different. Try composing a melody with rhythmic unity, but melodic variety. Try composing a melody with melodic unity and rhythmic variety. Remind the students that they are building up their compositional tool kit. *Unity* and *variety* should be balanced somewhat—in music and in all art. Discuss this with examples.

REFLECT and DISCUSS: Try to suggest an emotional connection as you finalize the melody—how does this make you feel? Sad, happy, excited, angry? Is it possible to make the melody change character without modifying the pitches (rhythm, dynamics, tempos, articulations)?

COMPOSE: Work on experimenting with a variety of rhythms for a given melody. Add dynamics, articulations, and tempo, and modify these elements while keeping the pitches the same. How do these changes affect the melody and its emotional impact?

COMPOSE: Add accompaniment to student melodies by using previous lessons.

COMPOSE/IMPROVISE: Create aleatoric music where students play their melody simultaneously with other students, but only when cued by the conductor.

GO THE EXTRA MILE

Create your own scale or small note set—for example: whole-tone scale; octatonic scale; unique scale you make up like DEGA; chromatic mixed with minor or major. Use the intervals whole, half, half, whole, half, half, and so on. Pick random pitches and make this your scale. Write a melody with your new scale. Encourage students who would like to do more work outside of class to visit the Music-COMP (Music Composition Mentoring Program, formerly the Vermont MIDI Project) website and listen to the audio lectures or read the PDF lessons of Erik Nielsen, professional composer. His first lesson is on the topic of "What makes an effective melody?"

NOTE

1. Carlos Santana, "Carlos Santana Quotes," BrainyQuote.com, retrieved December 16, 2019, https://www.brainyquote.com/quotes/carlos_santana_454474.

Chapter Five

Ostinato

Both work and play have a necessary place in children's education. . . . Play orients students to the engagement of their imagination. . . . Through play children learn to generate possibilities; manipulate symbols, sounds, images, and movements; and explore unique and uncharted paths without real-world consequences.

—John Kratus[1]

TEACHER GUIDE: LESSON 5. OSTINATO

> After completing this lesson, your students will be able to . . .
>
> Define *ostinato* and *syllable*.
> Create and perform a rhythmic ostinato (with the option to make it melodic as well).

Vocabulary Words

OSTINATO: A pattern of notes that is *repeated* many times and can be used to accompany other musical ideas. An ostinato is usually not longer than *one* or *two* measures, and can be *rhythmic* or *melodic* or *both*.
SYLLABLE: A part or whole of a word having one *vowel* sound.

Lesson Activities

See also Teacher Guide: Lesson 5. Ostinato: Supplemental Materials at the end of the chapter for suggestions.

PLAY a piece from your current repertoire that has an ostinato, or add an ostinato of your own to a well-known melody that the whole ensemble can play, such as "Twinkle, Twinkle, Little Star" or "Ode to Joy" or even "Mary Had a Little Lamb."

ASK the students if any of them know the musical name for a pattern of notes that is repeated over and over in a composition like they just performed.

After having experienced one through playing it with the ensemble, DISCUSS what the definition of OSTINATO is. ASK how many times the students think the ostinato should be repeated to qualify as an official ostinato.

DEFINE OSTINATO as a pattern of notes that is *repeated* many times and can be used to accompany other musical ideas. An ostinato is usually not longer than *one* or *two* measures, and can be *rhythmic* or *melodic* or *both*.

LISTEN to a piece of music that demonstrates OSTINATO, such as Ravel's *Bolero*, or use popular music or movie music, such as the theme from *Ghostbusters*, and point out the bass line ostinato. Identify whether the ostinato is just rhythmic or rhythmic and melodic.

ILLUSTRATE OSTINATO by playing another piece of repertoire at the level of your ensemble, such as the ones below (more examples at all grade levels in the supplementary section at the end of the chapter).

Band examples: Dana Wilson's "Sang," Brian Balmages's "Nevermore"
Orchestra examples: Gustav Holst's *The Planets*: Mars, Gustav Holst's *St. Paul Suite*, Movement 2

DISCUSS the characteristics of the OSTINATOS in the listening and in the repertoire: short, rhythmic, and/or melodic, not usually more than one or two measures.

COMPOSE a rhythmic OSTINATO based on words of a given theme, such as a FOOD THEME or SCHOOL THEME.

LEAD the students by EXAMPLE, asking them to repeat after you, speaking rhythmically: "Hot dogs, hot dogs," "Homework, homework," and then clap and speak them simultaneously. Finally, have students think the word in their mind, and clap the rhythm of the word without speaking it. Try other food names, such as "buttermilk pancake," "hamburgers," "taco," and "pineapple," or school ideas like "teachers and students," "afterschool practice," "Concerts are wonderful." Ask for a student volunteer to rhythmically say a food word or school idea of their own choice.

On the board write down two or three students' word choices. It is optional to add the traditional notation under the words. You may develop and compose a musical piece using only the written words with no traditional notation.

Sample Food Names Represented with Rhythmic Notation

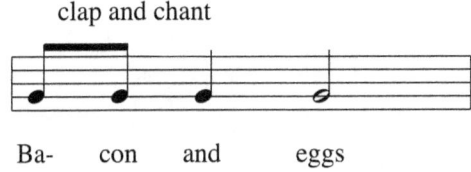

PRACTICE speaking, clapping, and playing the rhythms on instruments. Perform the ostinato on ONE pitch to start with, and then expand to TWO or THREE pitches. After performing the ostinato as an entire ensemble in unison, have students perform various ostinatos by assigning sections of the ensemble to one particular ostinato idea, and then cue the sections to start and stop visually.

DISCUSS the way words are transferred into rhythms, and then DEFINE SYLLABLE as a part or whole of a word having one VOWEL sound.

COMPOSE by having each student write down two or three food names that can be combined into a rhythmic OSTINATO similar to the examples shown above. ASK as many students as you have time for to speak or play their ostinato for the class. Select certain students' examples and write them on the board. PRACTICE each example as an entire ensemble, speaking, clapping and speaking, and finally performing on instruments.

DEVELOP the composition through solos, duets, layering, and mixing the ostinatos in various ways. Start with ostinatos on single pitches, but develop ostinatos with two or three pitches as time allows.

WRITE the words (ostinatos) on the board in the order the ensemble decides to finalize an "Ostinato Composition," and then PERFORM the composition through speaking, clapping, and playing it on instruments (or any combination thereof).

EXPAND this lesson by adding pitches to the ostinatos and adding melodies or other elements from the previous lessons. If you add pitches to the ostinato, encourage students to just use two or three pitches. Perform melodies from previous lessons with an ostinato composed from this lesson. Add a soundscape element. Mix and match previous concepts.

RECORD the piece; LISTEN and MODIFY it if you like.

RECORD/PERFORM the final group composition one more time, and LISTEN back to it, asking students again to evaluate what they like and don't like.

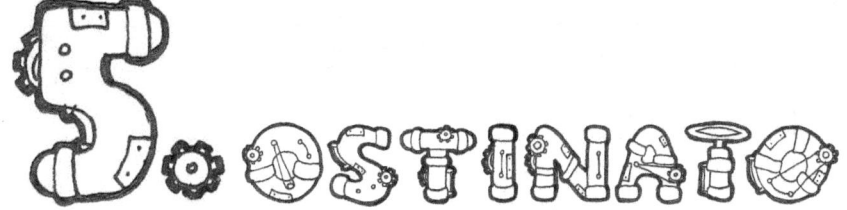

STUDENT WORKSHEET: LESSON 5. OSTINATO

Name: _____ Date: _____

Vocabulary

Ostinato: A pattern of notes that is _____ many times and can be used to accompany other musical ideas. An ostinato is usually not longer than _____ or _____ measures, and can be rhythmic or _____ or both.

Syllable: A part or whole of a word having one _____ sound.

Lesson Activities

Ostinato Composition

Create an OSTINATO by starting with a word or phrase, such as a food name (samples: hot dog, taco, buttermilk pancake). Write down TWO or THREE food names or combinations of names that you can play on your instrument. An example follows:

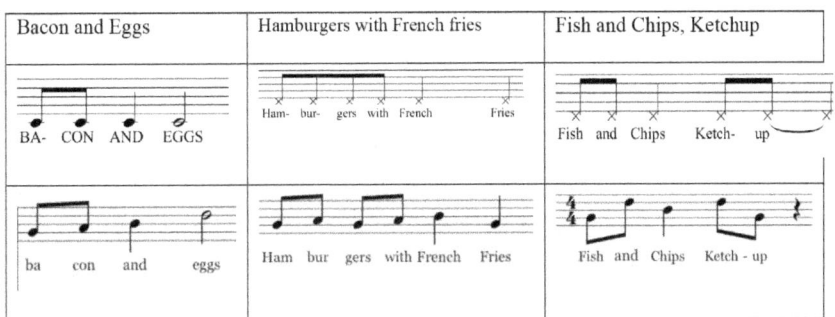

Food Ostinato Student Composition

	Fill in food name(s) or phrases in the blanks below.
1	
2	
3	

Step 2. OPTIONAL (ASK YOUR TEACHER IF YOU SHOULD DO THIS PART): Either below or on a separate piece of staff paper, write in the clef for your instruments (i.e., treble clef, alto clef, or bass clef). Write the words of your ostinato above the staff. Add the traditional musical notation on the staff. Add pitches (low, medium, high, or *do*, *re*, *mi*, etc., or as assigned by your teacher) and decide how many times to repeat the rhythm.

Additional option 1: Come up with a contrasting rhythm by thinking of a different food name.
Additional option 2: Improvise a solo while others play the ostinato.

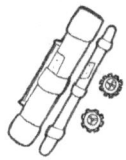

Ostinato

STUDENT WORKSHEET: LESSON 5. OSTINATO

Name: _____ Date: _____

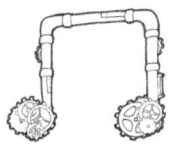

[Only this page authorized for duplication.]

TEACHER GUIDE: LESSON 5.
OSTINATO: SUPPLEMENTAL MATERIALS

OSTINATOS RECOMMENDED LISTENING

Maurice Ravel	*Bolero*
Gustav Mahler	Symphony no. 1, movement 3
Gustav Holst	*The Planets*, "Mars"
Igor Stravinsky	*The Rite of Spring*, Introduction and "Augurs of Spring"
Antonio Vivaldi	Violin Concerto in G Major (*La Stravaganza*), second movement
Elmer Bernstein	*Ghostbusters* (bass line ostinato)
John Williams	*Jaws*
Percy Mayfield	"Hit the Road Jack" (bass line ostinato)

Connection to Published Repertoire

SAMPLE REPERTOIRE WITH OSTINATOS

BAND

Kevin Lepper and Les Taylor	"Boomwhacker Bagatelle" (Grade 1)
Michael Story (Arr.)	"The Holly and the Ivy" (Grade 1)
Scott Watson	"El Cid" (Grade 1.5)
Brian West	"Fiesta" (Grade 2)
Dana Wilson	"Sang" (Grade 3)
Brian Balmages	"Nevermore" (Grade 3)
Gustav Holst	*Second Suite*, Movement 3, "Song of the Blacksmith" (Grade 4)

ORCHESTRA

Michael Story (Arr.)	"The Holly and the Ivy" (Grade 1)
Aaron Minsky	"Birds in Flight" (Grade 1)
Susan Day	"King's Court" (Grade 1.5)
Eugenia Goldman	"Journey" (Grades 1.5 to 2)
Soon Hee Newbold	"Dragon Dances" (Grade 2)
Doug Spata	"Gargoyles" (Grade 2)
Elliot Del Borgo	"*Canadian* Legend (Grade 3)
Gustav Holst	*St. Paul Suite*, Movement 2, Ostinato (Grade 4)

Lesson Activities

One way to extend this composition lesson is to work on using the expressive elements of DYNAMICS and ARTICULATIONS. As the students perform the rhythm of the word on their instruments, challenge them to add dynamics and articulations to give the ostinato additional character. Ask them, "Does this make it more interesting? What character or emotional changes can you produce with different articulation and dynamics?" What character does a taco have? "Spicy" loud, sharp, brittle. What character does a buttermilk pancake have? Soft, fluffy, syrupy, smooth; might be heavy, round, thick. Can you adjust your tone color, dynamics, and articulation to find the character of the word you are trying to perform? How can these expressive elements be used to enhance our ostinatos?

A second way to extend the composition lesson is to introduce DEVELOPMENT concepts of diminution, augmentation, inversion, retrograde, fragmentation, and sequence to develop the ostinato themes in different ways. Listening to Beethoven's Fifth Symphony is an exciting way to hear how a master composer develops a four-note motif.

COMPOSE a composition with ostinatos using only a single pitch, and focus on articulation, tempo, and dynamic changes for interest. DEVELOP the composition with diminution, augmentation, inversion, retrograde, fragmentation, and sequence. Optionally, layer in multiple ostinatos, each on a single, contrasting pitch, or add a limited set of pitches.

DISCUSS how to add tension and repose (dynamics, layering of ostinatos on top of one another, adding silence). Include tension and repose in the compositions.

Sample Composition 1: Mexican Food!

Text only, no traditional notation needed; limit to one pitch.

1. Starting food ostinato: Tacos, Tacos, Enchiladas, Beans.
2. Develop: Tacos (*p*), Tacos (*mp*), Tacos (*mf*), Enchiladas (*f*), Enchiladas (*ff*), Beans (*p*).
3. Contrasting foods introduced: Tostadas (triplet), Quesadillas, Tortillas.
4. Development: *Backward (Retrograde):* Tortillas, Quesadillas, Tostadas, Beans, Enchiladas, Tacos, Tacos. Double-time it (diminution), half-time it (augmentation), *mix it up*: Beans, Tacos, Enchiladas, Tacos, Tostadas. Beans, Tostadas; *random*: Tacos, Beans, Tostadas, Beans, Tacos, Enchiladas, Enchiladas, Enchiladas, Beans! *Simultaneous (layered)*: Brass or

violins perform "Taco, Taco" ostinato while woodwinds or low strings play "Tostadas, Tostadas," while percussion play "Beans, Enchiladas, Beans, Enchiladas." If you make "Tostadas" a triplet, it is a great opportunity to combine duple and triple simultaneously! And consider adding articulation and dynamics.

Sample Composition 2: Salmon Rolls!

(with pitches added)

If time allows, add the vocabulary word RIFF: A repeated group of notes used frequently in *rock* music and *jazz*, found in songs such as "Smoke on the Water" and "Sweet Child O' Mine."

RIFF RECOMMENDED LISTENING

Deep Purple	"Smoke on the Water"
Guns N' Roses	"Sweet Child O' Mine"
Charles Mingus	"Haitian Fight Song"
Herbie Hancock	"Bring Down the Birds"
Herbie Hancock	"Chameleon"
Pearl Jam	"Jeremy"
Black Sabbath	"Iron Man"

If time allows, connect to world music of your choice that uses ostinatos, such as "Guajeo."

See also "Ostinato," Wikipedia, http://en.wikipedia.org/wiki/Ostinato.

Marc Najjar, CMEBassment, "100 Bass Riffs: A Brief History of Groove on Bass and Drums," YouTube, September 12, 2014, https://youtu.be/T-RjmUFec40.

For a fun video diversion, watch this favorite YouTube example of a short ostinato being developed in multiple ways: "Anamaniacs—Wakko's 2 Note Song—Clip from Season 4," video, 4:39, posted June 19, 2014, https://www.youtube.com/watch?v=mA4AddSgfYQ.

In this video written by Peter Hastings and directed by Rusty Mills, from episode 82, Wakko proves to Dr. Scratchansniff that his song made of two notes is actual music.

GO THE EXTRA MILE

Pick an ostinato or a riff that an ensemble member has composed that you think could line up with a melody your ensemble knows. Have half the group play that ostinato. Have the other half the ensemble perform a melody from lesson 4 or a song from a method book, like "Swing Low, Sweet Chariot" or another tune of your choice.

Repeat as above, but instead of performing "Swing Low," layer other ostinato ideas or riffs on top of the base ostinato, giving space for starting and stopping various solo riffs/ostinatos while the root ostinato never stops. Options here include varying the instrumentation, solos, and range, building on previous lessons. Sample: *Urban Groove*, by John McAllister, available at https://www.johnmcallistermusic.com/uploads/2/4/7/2/24727629/urban_groove.pdf.[2]

NOTES

1. John Kratus, "The Roles of Work and Play in Music Education" (Paper presentation, Philosophy of Music Education International Symposium, Los Angeles, CA, 1997), 4.

2. John McAllister Music, https://www.johnmcallistermusic.com/, includes a blog, compositions, and more.

Chapter Six

Textures

Music, I feel, must be emotional first and intellectual second.
—Maurice Ravel[1]

I'm an adventurer. I like invention, I like discovery.
—Karlheinz Stockhausen[2]

TEACHER GUIDE: LESSON 6. TEXTURES

After completing this lesson, your students will be able to . . .

Define *texture*, especially in the musical sense.
Define *monophonic, polyphonic,* and *homophonic.*
Aurally distinguish between three types of musical texture.
Create any of the three specified textures in their own musical composition.

Vocabulary Words

TEXTURE: Refers to how music can sound *thick* or *thin* and how complex it sounds rhythmically, and harmonically, as detailed by the words below:

MONOPHONY: "*One* sound"; *one* melody line only; no accompaniment; can be more than one instrument or voice (thick) or a single instrument or voice (thin), as long as the *same* notes and rhythms are being played. In drama, a *monologue* is a speech given by one person.

> **TEACHER TIP**
>
> Remember to promote notation and recording software like Noteflight (free), MuseScore (free), Soundtrap® (free), and also Notion, Finale, Sibelius, Logic, GarageBand, and so on—as well as having traditional staff paper available in your rehearsal room for students to compose and arrange with anytime they get inspired! It is great to have some larger-size, spaced musical notation paper for those whose writing may not be as refined. Additionally, having some plain staff notation paper, as well as some staff score paper that is prepared with the standard band or orchestra instrumentation added, is helpful.

HOMOPHONY: One *melody* with accompaniment (i.e., chords or soundscape accompaniment). Most popular music styles like rock, folk, and country music use homophony. In pure homophony, all voices move in the same rhythm, as in hymn singing in church or a simple chorale.

POLYPHONY: "Many sounds"; *two* or more melodies, equally important, at the same time (the melodies should have different rhythms). Baroque music is all about polyphony.

Lesson Activities

*See also Teacher Guide: Lesson 6. Texture: Supplemental Materials at the end of the chapter for suggestions.

PREPARE students by playing short excerpts of music from your regular repertoire that represent monophonic (ensemble in unison and/or octaves), polyphonic (two or more melodies at once), and homophonic (one melody with accompaniment). Other than your regular repertoire, another easy way to do this is by having the ensemble play a scale in unison, then in two or three parts at different speeds, and then with one section only playing the scale while the other sections drone the tonic.

DISCUSS whether the sounds the ensemble played were *thick* or *thin*. DISCUSS how the rhythm, melody, and harmony can be a contributing factor to how thick or thin the music sounds. Different rhythms at the same time create a more complex and thicker sound, while single melodies with simple accompaniment sound thinner.

INTRODUCE the word *texture*. Have students physically touch and feel a variety of physical textures such as a music stand, their clothing, the floor, the soft inside covering on their instrument case. Have students imagine touching some more bizarre textures like dry bread with ice cream and fresh scrambled eggs, or imagine tea, butter, and yogurt mixed together. Describe the texture in terms of soft or hard, thick or thin, and simple or complex.

DISCUSS how these textures might be represented in music. Help students understand that this is different than orchestration or instrumentation, and remind them the term for that is *timbre*.

EXPLAIN that in music, we usually refer to three basic kinds of texture: monophony, polyphony, and homophony.

DEFINE *monophony* as "*one* sound" and one melody line only. Be clear that there is no accompaniment, though it can be more than one instrument or voice (thick) or a single instrument or voice (thin), so long as the *same* notes and rhythms are being played. (Playing an exercise from their method book in unison where everyone plays the same melody and rhythm—percussion on the bell part—is a great example of homophony.) ASK students what it is called in drama when one person gives a speech (answer: *monologue*).

ASK students to identify an example of a piece of music the ensemble played previously that was monophony, or ask one student to perform an example of monophony by playing their solo from the previous composition lesson.

DEFINE *polyphony* as two or more melodies performed at the same time. Stress that the melodies are equally important, and that the melodies should have different rhythms.

ASK students to identify an example of a piece of music the ensemble played previously that used polyphony (or was *polyphonic*), or ask two students to perform polyphony by playing their solos from the previous composition lesson together at the same time.

DEFINE *homophony* as one single melody that is leading the music, and other voices are accompanying (with chords, for example). Most popular music styles like rock, folk, and country music use homophony. Play a chorale or hymn as an example.

ASK students to identify an example of a piece of music the ensemble played previously that used homophony (or was *homophonic*), or have a student perform his or her melody from the previous lesson, while the rest of the ensemble plays a drone or rhythmic ostinato. Look for examples from your repertoire that are homophonic.

CREATE a composition together that has all three of these textures. You can use the student worksheet to engage all students in creating a group composition, and have everyone write down the composition as it evolves, or you

> **TEACHER TIP: NOTATION**
>
> NOTATION IS OPTIONAL: If you choose to have students notate the composition, ask them to draw the clef for their instrument on a piece of staff paper (treble clef, alto clef, or bass clef). Then, have them add the time signature, if they know it, and if they are not sure, that is fine as well. *Generally, adding notation decreases creativity, so consider leaving the notation out, unless students are already proficient at it.*
>
> Students could also use stick notation and solfège, if they have been taught that.

can lead a group composition as an example, and then ask individuals or small groups to create a new composition themselves based on the example completed in class.

Composition Part 1: Monophony

Students can vote on a melody from the previous melody lesson, the teacher can pick a melody, or a new original melody can be created in class. Students should vote on whether this first part should be performed with thick or thin texture (e.g., tutti, many people, or just a few) and what timbre they would like. Consider having students play the melody first as an entire ensemble, and then repeat it, alternating one section at a time from the ensemble (woodwinds, then percussion, etc.).

Composition Part 2: Homophony

ASK the students, "Now, what would you do to create homophony with this melody? How can we make it *homophonic?*"

STUDENTS choose and compose a drone or soundscape or an ostinato accompaniment.

For a SOUNDSCAPE example, teachers and students could use a creative soundscape, based on the first lesson. Students should take a minute and write down what they think would be a good accompaniment to the melody. One example could be finger snapping and saying "Shhhhhhh," which makes a nice accompaniment, like the sound of a gentle rain. Students should decide on what musical elements to use, such as THICK or THIN, and what TIMBRE, and they should VOTE on how the band members should perform the soundscape. The dynamic should be *piano*, because it is an accompaniment.

For an OSTINATO example, students could tap their pencils on their stand in an ostinato pattern from lesson 5. Again, students should vote on musical elements such as thick or thin texture and timbre and decide how the band members should perform the ostinato. Remind students the dynamic should be *piano*, because it is accompaniment.

Composition Part 3: Polyphony

ASK the students, "Now, what would you do to turn this composition into a polyphonic composition? How can we make it *polyphonic*?"

Consider all student ideas! Hopefully one or more will work! One easier (quick) option is to take the primary melody and perform it in a canon (like a round). Additionally, it could be sequenced to different pitch levels. For example it could be a canon at the interval of a fifth. Play the different canonic entrances in different keys. Also consider having two students perform polyphony by playing two completely different melodies simultaneously, or compose a new melody to go against the primary melody. (Point out to the students that this is a THIN polyphonic texture). Try three to five or more people playing different melodies all at once. (Note that this is a THICK polyphonic texture.)

PRACTICE AND PERFORM: Combine and perform all three parts as one composition. Consider building tension during the polyphonic third part and incorporating a sense of release or repose to end the piece, and/or bring out the concepts of unity and variety. Consider unity, through the melody, and variety, through the timbre and texture.

The supplementary materials include a texture listening exercise followed by test 2, which covers lessons 4–6.

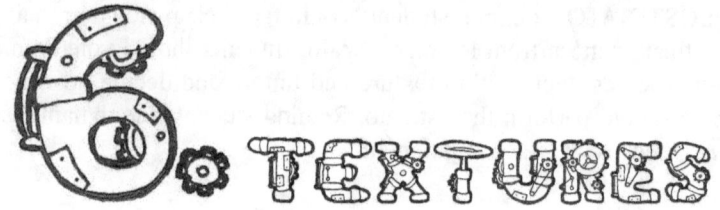

STUDENT WORKSHEET: LESSON 6. TEXTURES

Name: _____ Date: _____

Vocabulary

Texture: Describes how music can sound _____ or _____ and how complex it sounds rhythmically and harmonically.

Monophony: "_____ sound"; _____ melody line; no accompaniment; can be more than one instrument or voice (thick) or a single instrument or voice (thin), as long as the _____ notes and rhythms are being played.

Homophony: One _____ with chords accompanying. Most popular music styles like rock, folk, and country music use homophony. In pure homophony, all voices move in the same rhythm.

Polyphony: "Many sounds"; _____ or more melodies at the same time (the melodies should have different rhythms).

Lesson Activities

CREATE a composition in three parts, with monophony, homophony, and polyphony.

Optional notation: If your teacher asks you to notate your composition, draw the clef for your instrument on a piece of staff paper (treble clef, alto clef, or bass clef). If you know the meter (4/4 or 3/4 or 2/4, etc.), add that to the staff. Then notate your composition.

Composition Part 1: Monophony

Compose a short and simple melody or use a melody composed by your teacher or class. Consider using a melody from the previous melody lesson. Play it as a solo (thin), or have many play the melody together in unison (thick).

Composition Part 2. Homophony

Now, what would you do to create homophony with the melody from part 1? Consider a drone, or *soundscape*, or compose an *ostinato* that you would like to use to accompany the class-chosen melody (melody and accompaniment). Note the dynamic should be *piano*, because it is an accompaniment.

Soundscape or *ostinato?* Thick or thin? Timbre? Describe it here:

Composition Part 3. Polyphony

Now, using the melodic material from parts 1 and/or 2, what would you do to turn this section of the composition into a polyphonic composition? Write your ideas here:

Name: _____ Date: _____

Monophony, Homophony, Polyphony Composition: Title (optional):
_____

Texture Listening Exercise—Your teacher will play five different music examples. Circle the correct responses below.

Note that you could circle different numbers depending on how thin or thick you hear the texture to be. Use "1" for very thin, like a solo instrument playing, and use "10" for very thick, like a large band or orchestra playing, or two or more melodies simultaneously, or multiple complex rhythms all at once (poly rhythmic).

For the *monophony*, *homophony*, and *polyphony* choices, try to circle which one represents the PRIMARY texture as demonstrated by the audio excerpt.

Sample: "Amazing Grace," sung solo and a capella: circle "Thin 1" and "monophony," because it is a single melody without accompaniment.

Texture Listening Exercise

Circle one: *1 is very thin and 10 is very thick*	*Circle one:*
1. Thin 1 2 3 4 5 6 7 8 9 10 Thick	Monophony Homophony Polyphony
2. Thin 1 2 3 4 5 6 7 8 9 10 Thick	Monophony Homophony Polyphony
3. Thin 1 2 3 4 5 6 7 8 9 10 Thick	Monophony Homophony Polyphony
4. Thin 1 2 3 4 5 6 7 8 9 10 Thick	Monophony Homophony Polyphony
5. Thin 1 2 3 4 5 6 7 8 9 10 Thick	Monophony Homophony Polyphony

[Only this page authorized for duplication.]

TEACHER GUIDE: LESSON 6.
TEXTURES: SUPPLEMENTAL MATERIALS

Recommended Listening for Texture

Texture Listening Exercise Samples—Optional Assessment Tool
Play musical audio examples and have students fill in the student handout by labeling whether each is example is thick or thin, monophony, polyphony, or homophony. (See student handout.) Be sure to prepare each example in advance so you are clear on what possible answer students will circle. The examples below are only a sample of the huge variety of works that could be presented. Each teacher is encouraged to pick a variety of styles and genres of music they feel would be good to share with their students.

TEXTURE LISTENING SUGGESTIONS (SEE STUDENT HANDOUT)

1. Olivier Messiaen, *Quartet for the End of Time*—"Abyss of the Birds." Solo clarinet. THIN, MONOPHONY.

   Other suggestions: "Simple Gifts" (traditional), as performed by Yo-Yo Ma; Ludwig van Beethoven, "Ode to Joy" excerpt theme from Symphony no. 9. THIN; MONOPHONY/POLYPHONY.

2. Gustav Mahler: Symphony no. 3—opening with horns only. MEDIUM THIN, because it is just horns, but there are eight of them; MONOPHONIC.

   Other suggestions: Bon Jovi, "Living on a Prayer." THICK, HOMOPHONIC.

3. Johann Sebastian Bach, chorales. THIN or THICK, HOMOPHONY.

   Other suggestions: Holst, *Mars*, starts THIN, grows THICK, HOMOPHONY, POLYPHONY.

4. Anthony Plog, *Animal Ditties VII for Brass Quintet*—6. "The Octopus." Brass quintet; MEDIUM THICK, POLYPHONY (listen for multiple melodies simultaneously, plus voice).

   Other suggestions: John Williams, *Star Wars*; Howard Shore, *Lord of the Rings*—"Minas Morgul." THICK, POLYPHONIC. Johann Sebastian Bach, Two-Part Invention. THIN—only one instrument, but two parts / left and right hand, POLYPHONIC—two melodies.

   Other suggestions: Karl King, "The Melody Shop." THIN TO THICK; POLYPHONIC AND HOMOPHONIC.

Also: Use examples for your own ensemble literature. Have everyone play a piece together, then each person must label on their student handout whether the example they just performed was thick or thin, monophony, polyphony, or homophony. Consider giving a homework assignment that involves students' listening to one of their favorite pieces and reporting back on the texture.

Connection to Published Repertoire

SAMPLE REPERTOIRE FOR TEXTURES

BAND

Jody Blackshaw's "Whirlwind" (Grade 1) starts with a soundscape, and then has solos (thin, monophonic), tutti ensemble (thick), canon (polyphonic), and tutti ensemble together (homophonic), and is a representation of all the components of this texture composition lesson.

Bob Margolis's "Two Minute Symphony" (Grade 1.5) shows off bass instruments as well as treble instruments and has a big exciting sound.

Timothy Broege's "The Headless Horseman" (Grade 2) can be used to teach many aspects of this lesson: euphonium solo, trumpet solo with mute, trombones sliding at the opening, and so on.

John Carnahan's ". . . And the Antelope Play" (Grade 3) uses a huge variety of textures, including monophonic, homophonic, and polyphonic. There are solos (thin texture) as well as tuttis, and creative combinations of instruments as well, offering inspiring texture examples for young composers. This piece is also perfect for tying back to the first lesson on soundscapes.

Michael Colgrass's "Old Churches" (Grade 3) includes aluminum bowls and melodies inspired by Gregorian chant. A variety of textures, thick and thin, are used, as well as a creative orchestration that features various sections of the band. The aleatoric approaches connect well with the soundscape lesson as well (chapter 1).

ORCHESTRA

Elliot Del Borgo's "Pentatonic Overture" (Grade 1) is *perfect* for discussing texture and inspiring young composers to experiment with different textures. The piece uses unison playing (monophonic), as well as homophonic and polyphonic sections.

Bob Phillips's "Sword Dance" (Grade 1) for full orchestra includes the melody for every section at various times, and each variation is presented with a different texture and accompaniment.

Richard Meyer's "Ear-igami" (Grade 2) involves tom-tom and wind chimes, as well as paper, and is great way to introduce creative textures as a composing concept for students.

Mary Alice Rich's "Hunted" (Grade 3) conveys its tension with the interplay of eighth note thematic phrases volleyed between voices. At some point, everyone gets to play the theme. This is a great teaching piece for texture because it not only includes thin and thick, polyphonic and homophonic, but it also has a brief col legno section that adds texture and a suspenseful special effect.

Lesson Activities

The English word *texture* used in the context of music is fascinating because it means the overall type of sound in combinations of orchestration, but it also refers to monophony, polyphony, and homophony. When discussing polyphony, consider adding the word *counterpoint* to the vocabulary list. It is very much like polyphony and means basically the same thing, though advanced students might enjoy a brief introduction to the old classic rules of *species counterpoint*. The adjective *contrapuntal* is also frequently used to describe music with two or more melodies simultaneously. The adjectives *monophonic*, *homophonic*, and *polyphonic* should go hand in hand with their noun counterparts.

Ideas for Examples of Different Textures

Homophony: Everyone snaps his or her fingers and says, "Shhhhhhh" while a soloist plays a melody from a previous lesson or improvises. Use soundscape ideas from lesson 1 and/or timbre ideas from lesson 2. Alternately, woodwinds could play a major tonic chord while brass play "Ode to Joy." If using a method book with unison exercises, have one part of the ensemble play the unison exercise while the rest of the ensemble does a soundscape accompaniment. Play chorales or hymns from a method book or concert piece.

Composition Tips

For the Composition Part 1, Monophony

If you are short on time, ideally just pick out a student melody from the previous lessons and have it ready for the class, transposed for all appropriate instruments. If that is not possible, consider using a famous melody everyone knows, such as "Ode to Joy" or "Frère Jacques." This will teach the concepts of this lesson without your having to spend time composing a new melody. If you have more time, students could listen to the way Beethoven treats "Ode to Joy" in the last movement of the Ninth Symphony and the way Mahler treats "Frère Jacques" in the slow movement of his First Symphony. These are examples of thick and thin texture, monophonic, homophonic, and polyphonic.

If you do have time to develop a new melody, consider these suggestions:

A. Use the first three to five notes of a major scale, such as B-flat major (band) or D major (orchestra). Remind any students who wonder about

only using five notes that Beethoven only used five notes for the "Ode to Joy" theme, and it is one of the most famous melodies ever written in the entire world!
B. Consider using a rhythm from lesson 3 (rhythm) or 5 (ostinato) or creating a new interesting rhythm
C. Try to limit the melody to fit on a single staff. Consider adding a repeat sign or "da capo" at the end, and have the melody played once by the whole ensemble and once by a soloist or section.

For the Composition Part 2, Homophony

Explore several of the students' creative ideas, or encourage them with ideas like the following: (1) Pick several soloists who take turns playing melodies. (2) Experiment with various accompaniments, such as flutes playing B-flat quietly while everyone else wiggles their valves or keys, drones from low instruments, or provides a percussion ostinato throughout.

For the Composition Part 3, Polyphony

Consider ending with something like a cymbal crash or bass drum roll to a tutti ensemble "hit" to get a fun ending with everyone involved. For example, explain, "To end, the conductor will point to the bass drum and suspended cymbal players who will crescendo until the conductor gives the final cue; on the final cue everyone pick your favorite note and play it as loud and short as possible!" Always encourage students to think about the different options, try different options, and then vote on which one to perform for the final composition performance. Ask questions such as, "Will this be a thick texture on the last note, or thin?"

TEST 2: LESSONS 4–6. MELODY, OSTINATO, AND TEXTURES

Name: _____ Date: _____

Match the following words with their correct definition by writing the correct letter in the blank:

1. _____ Ostinato
2. _____ Improvising
3. _____ Syllable
4. _____ Texture
5. _____ Monophony
6. _____ Polyphony
7. _____ Homophony

A. A pattern of notes that is repeated many times and can be used to accompany other musical ideas
B. How music can sound thick or thin and how complex music sounds rhythmically and harmonically
C. "One sound"; one melody line only; no accompaniment
D. A part or whole of a word having one vowel sound
E. Two or more melodies, equally important, at the same time
F. One melody with chords accompanying
G. Masking up music on the spot without planning it out or writing it down

9. Write a food name and then show how that food name could translate into music by writing it with traditional notation or demonstrating it on your instrument. (Use the back of this paper if you need more room).

Identify the following audio examples that your teacher will play for you as either thick, thin, monophony, homophony, or polyphony—circle your answers below.

Listening for Texture

Test 2: Questions 10 to 12: Listening for Texture

Circle one: 1 is very thin and 10 is very thick	Circle one:
10. Thin 1 2 3 4 5 6 7 8 9 10 Thick	Monophony Homophony Polyphony
11. Thin 1 2 3 4 5 6 7 8 9 10 Thick	Monophony Homophony Polyphony
12. Thin 1 2 3 4 5 6 7 8 9 10 Thick	Monophony Homophony Polyphony

[Only this page authorized for duplication.]

TEACHER ANSWER KEY: TEST 2. LESSONS 4–6

Matching:

1. A   Ostinato
2. G   Improvising
3. D   Syllable
4. B   Texture
5. C   Monophony
6. E   Polyphony
7. F   Homophony

A. A pattern of notes that is repeated many times and can be used to accompany other musical idea
B. How music can sound thick or thin and how complex music sounds rhythmically and harmonically
C. "One sound"; one melody line only; no accompaniment
D. A part or whole of a word having one vowel sound
E. Two or more melodies, equally important, at the same time
F. One melody with chords accompanying
G. Making up music on the spot without planning it out or writing it down

Question 9. Samples:

Sample Food Ostinatos

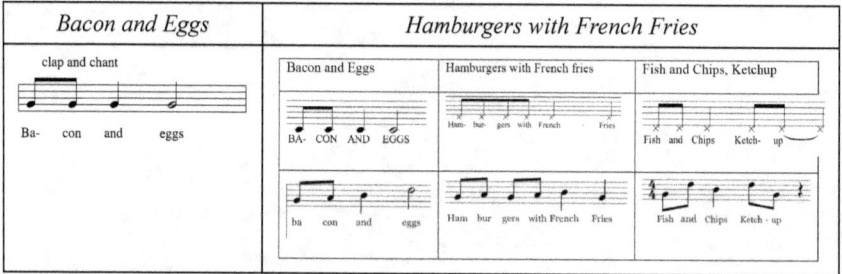

The answers to questions 10–12 are left open for the teacher's own audio example choices. Each teacher may circle their own appropriate answers below to fill in the official answers for grading the student tests.

Test 2: Questions 10 to 12: Answers

Circle one: *1 is very thin and 10 is very thick*	*Circle one:*
Name of piece: _____ 10. Thin 1 2 3 4 5 6 7 8 9 10 Thick	Monophony Homophony Polyphony
Name of piece: _____ 11. Thin 1 2 3 4 5 6 7 8 9 10 Thick	Monophony Homophony Polyphony
Name of piece: _____ 12. Thin 1 2 3 4 5 6 7 8 9 10 Thick	Monophony Homophony Polyphony

NOTES

1. "Maurice Ravel," Conductor's Corner, accessed December 12, 2019, http://conductorscorner.org/public_html/Ravel/Entries/2018/10/5_RAVEL_QUOTES.html.

2. Karlheinz Stockhausen, "Karlheinz Stockhausen Quotes," AllGreatQuotes, accessed December 12, 2019, https://www.allgreatquotes.com/quote-269545/.

Chapter Seven

Text-Based Composing

Ah, music, a magic beyond all we do here!

—Albus Dumbledore[1]

Lyrics have to be underwritten. That's why poets generally make poor lyric writers because the language is too rich. You get drowned in it.

—Stephen Sondheim[2]

TEACHER GUIDE: LESSON 7. TEXT-BASED COMPOSING

> After completing this lesson, your students will be able to . . .
>
> Define *melody, rhythm, syllable,* and *word painting.*
> Create and perform a composition based on a poem using two tools:
> 1. Translating syllables into rhythm—deriving rhythm from words, and
> 2. Using text painting to capture the character, meaning, or emotion of the words.

Vocabulary Words

MELODY: A series of musical *tones* that are grouped together to create a single musical idea, or a "musical sentence."
RHYTHM: A pattern of *beats* in music.
SYLLABLE: A part or whole of a *word* having one vowel sound (from lesson 5).

STRESSED: A word or syllable that is spoken with *more* emphasis, through louder speech volume, longer length, or higher pitches.

UNSTRESSED: A word or syllable that is spoken with *less* emphasis, through less volume, shorter length, or lower pitch.

WORD OR TEXT PAINTING: An attempt with *music* to represent a certain word or words in a text. The music tries to imitate the character, meaning, or *emotion* of the text. For example, for the word *sunrise*, the composer could choose to have rising musical lines, maybe upward moving scales, representing the sun rising up in the sky. To represent *anger*, a composer might choose very loud, accented, dissonant chords.

Lesson Activities

See also Teacher Guide: Lesson 7. Text-Based Composing: Supplemental Materials at the end of the chapter for suggestions.

Overview of Lesson 7

Part 1: Learning from Mozart
Part 2: Preparing for Composing with Text
Part 3: Composing Music Based on a Selected Text

Part 1: Learning from Mozart

READ the Latin and then the English translation of the text of Mozart's Requiem in D Minor, K 626–3, *Sequentia: Dies Irae* with the students.

Mozart *Requiem* Lyrics: *Dies Irae*

Original Latin	English Translation
Dies irae, Dies illa	Day of wrath! O day of mourning!
Solvet saeclum en favlilla	See fulfilled the prophets' warning,
Teste davidcum sybilla	Heaven and earth in ashes burning!

Discuss Mozart's text first—DON'T listen to the music yet!! The poem describes the *Day of Judgment*, when the last trumpet summons souls before the throne of God, where the saved will be delivered and the unsaved cast into eternal flames.

ASK students, "If you were the composer, how would you try to capture those words using music?" Ask students to write down their responses to how they think the following musical elements might be used to represent the text: Dynamics? Tempo? Articulation? Instrumentation? Range? For example, should *Dies Irae* be loud (forte) or soft (piano)? Should the instrumentation be many players (thick) including brass, woodwinds, and strings, or just a solo violin or clarinet (thin)?

LISTEN to a recording and ask students to consider whether Mozart was successful in capturing the text. On the student worksheet, ask students to circle all the answers that they think are correct as they listen to the music.

After listening, DISCUSS with students whether they think Mozart captured the spirit of the lyrics effectively and why. Have them write down their ideas.

Part 2: Preparing for Composing with Text

REVIEW the concepts of melody and rhythm (student worksheet, fill in the blanks). MELODY: A series of musical *tones* that are grouped together to create a single musical idea, or a "musical sentence."

RHYTHM: A pattern of *beats* in music.

REFLECT with the students on how the melody and rhythm that Mozart composed were matched to the text (e.g., jumpy melody appropriate for "day of wrath"; rhythms were also fast and varied to bring out the text).

REVIEW the other vocabulary on the student worksheet.

SYLLABLE: A part or whole of a *word* having one vowel sound.
STRESSED: A word or syllable that is spoken with *more* emphasis, through louder speech volume, longer length, or higher pitches.
UNSTRESSED: A word or syllable that is spoken with *less* emphasis, through less volume, shorter length, or lower pitch.
WORD OR TEXT PAINTING: An attempt with music to represent a certain word or words in a text. The music tries to imitate the character, meaning, or *emotion* of the text. For example, for the word *sunrise*, the composer could choose to have rising musical lines, maybe upward moving scales, representing the sun rising up in the sky. To represent *anger*, a composer might choose very loud, accented, dissonant chords. (Ask students if they noticed if Mozart did this.)

Point out how, not only does the character and emotion of the text come out, but also the SYLLABLES of the text are rhythmically set in a natural way. Speak the words "Dies irae, Dies illa, Solvet saeclum" and then listen again to how Mozart set the rhythm of the words to line up with the syllables correctly and bring out the meaning.

Part 3: Composing Music Based on a Selected Text

One example is given here, and others can be found in "Teacher Guide: Lesson 7. Text-Based Composing: Supplemental Materials" section after the student worksheet.

Proverb: *A gentle answer turns away wrath, but a harsh word stirs up anger.* (Proverbs 15:1)

DERIVE the musical rhythm of this proverb based on the syllables of the text.

Try to help the students figure out the time signature and figure out the rhythm of these words on their own.

1. SOUND OUT THE SYLLABLES by speaking them out loud together as a class. Encourage students to be expressive!
2. CLAP and SPEAK the text simultaneously to really clarify the rhythmic aspects of the words.
3. DRAW vertical lines for each syllable on the board below the syllable, representing the rhythms of the words and phrase. Add stems and bars to the vertical lines to finalize a RHYTHM for the text. (The teacher can do this on the board, or students can do it on their handout.)
4. Over the top of the rhythm, add PHRASE markings that line up with the flow and structure of the text.
5. Figure out if there is a TIME SIGNATURE that makes sense with the rhythmic flow and notate this.
6. Draw in BAR LINES.
7. Compose a MELODY. Build on the previous melody lesson by using the first five notes of a scale, and use these tones for this composition. Have students start by improvising melodies on their instrument and continue until they are happy with the way the melody sounds. Notate the melody on the board or help the students notate on their individual papers as needed.
8. Choose TIMBRE (instrumentation). What instruments would you use to characterize the text? (Think about text painting; unity, variety; tutti, solo, duet, trio, etc.)
9. Assign DYNAMICS. (See appendix 1, "Dynamics and Articulation Charts" at the end of the book.) To represent the text, should the music be loud or soft or in-between? Crescendo, diminuendo?
10. Consider ARTICULATION. (See appendix 1, "Dynamics and Articulation Charts" at the end of the book.) Should the music be staccato or legato? Accented? Mixed?
11. Select TEMPO and character description. Is it fast (allegro) or slow (adagio) or does it change? For example, you might label the tempo as

"Andante moderato" or "Medium slow, with great feeling" or "Fast and furious."

12. REFLECT: What other text painting could we do to musically describe the text? Consider whether any words or emotions should be represented using text painting. Help students explore various options as time allows.
13. Consider adding an ACCOMPANIMENT that supports the text. Maybe add a *soundscape* accompaniment or an *ostinato*, or keep a *monophonic* melody, or maybe create a canon and turn the piece into a *polyphonic* composition. Consider whether the text should be performed speaking or singing simultaneously with the composed music or alternating with the music, or whether the composition will be purely instrumental.
14. If you have time, RECORD, LISTEN, and REVISE. Help the student reflect on their composition. What did they like about it? Not like? How could it be developed or changed? Should we add any rests? Should we repeat? Maybe repeat with a different timbre? How is the range? Is the texture working well or should it be varied? Should we add a sequence? Should we develop the melody through augmentation? Diminution? Fragmentation?

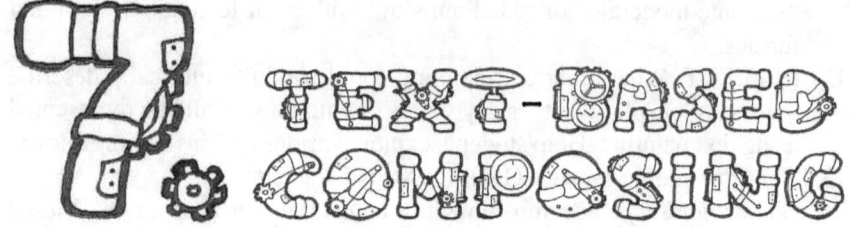

Chapter Seven

STUDENT WORKSHEET:
LESSON 7. TEXT-BASED COMPOSING

Name: _____ Date: _____

Vocabulary

Melody: A series of musical _____ that are grouped together to make a single musical idea or "musical sentence."

Rhythm: A pattern of _____ in music.

Syllable: A part or whole of a _____ having one vowel sound.

Stressed: A word or syllable that is spoken with _____ emphasis, through louder speech volume, longer length, or higher pitches.

Unstressed: A word or syllable that is spoken with _____ emphasis, through less volume, shorter length, or lower pitch.

Word or text painting: An attempt with _____ to represent a certain word or words in a text. The music tries to imitate the character, meaning, or _____ of the text. For example, for the word *sunrise*, the composer could choose to have rising musical lines, maybe upward moving scales, representing the sun rising up in the sky. To represent *anger*, a composer might choose very loud, accented, dissonant chords.

Lesson Activities

READ the Latin and then the English translation of Mozart's *Requiem In D Minor, K 626–3. Sequentia, Dies Irae*.

Mozart *Requiem* Lyrics: *Dies Irae*

Original Latin	English Translation
Dies irae, Dies illa	Day of wrath! O day of mourning!
Solvet saeclum en favlilla	See fulfilled the prophets' warning,
Teste davidcum sybilla	Heaven and earth in ashes burning!

If you were the composer, how would you try to capture those words in music? Please fill in your answers here:

Dynamics?

Tempo?

Articulation (accents, staccato, marcato, legato, etc.)?

Timbres/instrumentation?

Range?

Other musical ideas/description?

STUDENT WORKSHEET: LESSON 7.
MOZART'S *REQUIEM: DIES IRAE*—LISTENING

Name: _____ Date: _____

Now listen to a performance of what Mozart wrote and circle his choices:

Mozart's *Requiem: Dies Irae*—Listening Worksheet
You may circle more than one word in each category, but try to circle words that represent the PRIMARY musical concept for this music.

A. Dynamics?	Piano	Mezzo Piano	Mezzo Forte	Forte	Double Forte
B. Tempo?	Slow	Medium Slow	Medium Fast	Fast	
C. Articulation?		Gentle/Legato		Marcato (Slightly Separated) Staccato / Crisp / Biting	
D. Emotion?	Happy	Mellow	Angry	Other:	
E. Timbre?	Brass	Woodwinds	Strings	Percussion	
F. Range?	Low	Middle		High	

Do you think Mozart captured the spirit of the lyrics effectively? Why? Write your answer here:

Compose!

Use the following directions to create a new composition based on a selected text from your teacher. Compose a rhythm for your text based on the syllables of the text. Write the words here and then notate the rhythm underneath the words.

1. Sound out the syllables by speaking them out loud. Be expressive!
2. Next clap and speak the text with your class or composition team to try to get a feel for the rhythm that fits the text best.
3. Draw vertical lines for *each* syllable below the syllable, representing the rhythm. Add stems and bars to the vertical lines to finalize a rhythm for the text.
4. Add phrase markings over the top of the rhythm that line up with the flow and structure of the text.
5. Figure out if there is a time signature that makes sense with the rhythmic flow and write the time signature into the music.
6. Mark in bar lines.
7. Compose a melody: Either as a class or individually, using the notes of a scale your teacher assigns, and use the rhythm from your text. Practice this melody on your instrument and improvise until you are happy with the way the melody sounds. If your teacher asks you to notate the melody, write it on the staff on the next page.
8. Choose timbre: What instruments would you use to characterize the text? (Think about text painting; unity, variety, tutti, solo, duet, trio, etc.)
9. Assign dynamics: To represent the text, should the music be loud or soft or in-between? Crescendo, diminuendo?
10. Consider articulation: Should the notes be tenuto, staccato, or legato? Accented? Mixed?
11. Select a tempo and character description. Is it fast (allegro) or slow (adagio) or does it change? For example, you might label the tempo as "Andante Moderato" or "Medium slow, with great feeling" or "Fast and furious."
12. Reflect: What other text painting could we do to musically describe the text? Consider whether any words or emotions should be represented using text painting. Describe your ideas here; then add them to the composition. Ask your teacher for help if needed.

13. Consider an accompaniment: Maybe add a soundscape accompaniment or an ostinato, keep a monophonic melody, or maybe create a canon and turn the piece into a polyphonic composition. Consider whether the text should be performed speaking or singing simultaneously with the composed music or alternating with the music, or whether the composition will be purely instrumental. Should there be a musical introduction or postlude of any sort? Write your ideas here and add notes to your staff paper if your teacher is having you notate this composition.

14. Record, listen back, and revise, if you have time. Reflect on your composition: What did you like about it? Not like? How could it be developed or changed? Should we add any rests? Should we repeat? Maybe repeat with a different timbre? How is the range? Is the texture working well or should it be varied? Should we add a sequence? Should we develop the melody through augmentation? Diminution? Fragmentation?

Write any ideas down here:

[Only this page authorized for duplication.]

Title: _____
Lyrics by: _____
Music by: _____

[Only this page authorized for duplication.]

TEACHER GUIDE: LESSON 7. TEXT-BASED COMPOSING: SUPPLEMENTAL MATERIALS

TEXT-BASED COMPOSING RECOMMENDED LISTENING

In addition to Mozart's Requiem in D Minor, K 626–3: "Sequentia: Dies Irae," there are many famous pieces of music with lyrics for solo voice or choir and orchestra or band. Consider classical art songs, operas, and oratorios as well as pop music and hip hop. If possible, compare several settings of the same text to see how various composers treat text in different ways. Here are a few diverse examples:

Beethoven, Ludwig van	Ninth Symphony (choir, soloists, orchestra)
Berlioz, Hector	Symphony Fantastique (story told through music)
Colgrass, Michael	Winds of Nagual (wind ensemble work inspired by stories of Carlos Castaneda, Mexican sorcerer; good examples of text painting and descriptive music inspired by text)
Copland, Aaron	Lincoln Portrait (narrator with band or orchestra)
Debussy, Claude	Prelude to the Afternoon of a Faun (poem captured in music)
Goldsberry, Renée Elise	"Satisfied," from Hamilton (Broadway hit; includes a variety of styles, including singing and rapping)
Hill, Patty and Mildred J.	"Happy Birthday" (song)
Mahler, Gustav	"Um Mitternacht" (solo voice with chamber winds)
Plog, Anthony	"Animal Ditties" (narrator with brass quintet)
Prokofiev, Sergei	Peter and the Wolf (narrator with orchestra)
Reich, Steve	Different Trains (words from interviews put directly into the string quartet pre-recorded track and then imitated by the string instruments themselves)
Shaw, Caroline	Partita for 8 Voices (Pulitzer Prize winner; a capella)
Wolfe, Julia	Fire in My Mouth (for orchestra and voices)

SAMPLE REPERTOIRE: TEXT-BASED COMPOSING

REPERTOIRE CONNECTIONS

There are many instrumental pieces that are either settings of text-based pieces or inspired by text. Here are a few ideas to get you started! If a band or orchestra piece is based on a song with a text, always try to get the students to actually sing the original song together if at all possible. Often you can find both band and orchestra arrangements of the pieces listed here.

BAND

Balent, Andrew   "Amazing Grace" (Grade 1)
A famous song all students should know!

Piunno, Nicole   "Peanut Butter Jam" (Grade 1)
This fun, beginning band piece is simply inspired by the text "Peanut Butter Jam." Students get to shout/chant the words "crunchy" or "creamy" in the middle, in rhythm, offering a direct connection to your composing lesson on text and lining syllables up with rhythm.

Broege, Timothy   "The Headless Horseman" (Grade 2)
Broege was inspired by the story of Washington Irving's headless horseman in "The Legend of Sleepy Hollow." This piece opens with a soundscape that is a great example for young composers trying to catch the spirit and feelings of a story. It also has dramatic use of silence, 5/4 and 4/4 time signatures, and rhythms that represent the horse galloping.

Jolley, Jennifer   "Think About It" (Grade 2.5)
This catchy band piece is based on the funk tune by soul singer Lyn Collins. Students will enjoy the tune and may be inspired to take one of their own favorite pop tunes and compose a new version for your school ensemble.

Ticheli, Frank   *Simple Gifts* (Grade 3)
Includes "'Tis a gift to be simple." Have students reflect on how the music reflects the character and feelings of the lyrics.

Balmages, Brian   "Nevermore" (Grade 3)
Inspired by Edgar Allen Poe's poem "The Raven," this is a dramatic and creative work that will help students see how a composer can bring out the emotions of a poem even though the music doesn't use any words.

Bach, J. S.   "Come Sweet Death" (Grade 3+)
This band classic is based on a Bach chorale with the text "Komm, süsser Tod." Various arrangements are available.

Whitacre, Eric   "Lux Aurumque" (Grade 4)
This work was originally a choral work transcribed for band. Students (and teachers!) can learn a lot from studying how the composer adapted the choral music into the band setting, noting in particular how words are set to create certain feelings and noting how the text might affect the phrasing of the instrumental arrangement

ORCHESTRA

Handel, G. F., arr. Richard Meyer   "Hallelujah" chorus from *Messiah* (Grade 1)
This arrangement is for full orchestra, and Handel's exemplary treatment of the text makes this a perfect example for a composition lesson on setting text.

Monday, Deborah Baker "African Blessing" (Grade 1)

This arrangement of the Swahili song "Bwana Awabariki" gives young string players the chance to explore African culture and offers the opportunity to see how syllables of words in another language can translate into fun, catchy, rhythmically driven music.

Mozart, W. A., arr. Elliot Del Borgo. "Ave Verum Corpus" (Grade 2)

Mozart's masterwork is another gem for composition lessons on setting text to music. In particular, notice the climax toward the end where Mozart set the words "In mortis examine" (In trials of death) and point out to students how the word *death* is held out and extended, including leading to the highest note (soprano voice) of the whole piece.

Perry, Katy and Minaj, Nicki, arr. Victor López "Teenage Dream / Super Bass Mash-Up" (Grade 2.5)

This medley combines two tunes from hip hop and pop music that students will immediately recognize in the mash-up format combining parts of each tune from Katy Perry and Nicki Minaj.

Bernstein, Leonard, arr. John Moss "Somewhere" (from *West Side Story*) (Grade 3)

This famous song by Bernstein offers a great lesson for young composers to experience an emotional and powerful setting of an inspiring text. Lessons on jumps, skips, and steps as well as harmony, unity, and contrast are all ready for study in this melody.

Miranda, Lin-Manuel, arr. Jerry Brubaker. Suite from *Hamilton* (Grade 3.5)

This suite has six of the most musical selections from the show, including: "You'll Be Back," "Helpless," "My Shot," "Dear Theodosia," "It's Quiet Uptown," and "One Last Time."

Lesson Activities

Deciding on a text for this lesson will be one of the most important preparatory steps. Use any of the following poems and follow the same steps listed in this lesson. It is easy to just do one line of a poem and come up with the rhythm from the word syllables, and do a soundscape for the rest of the poem. Always consider the option of ending with the opening rhythm to create unity. Try to find a way to do at least a little text painting. Consider texts that naturally encourage exciting musical expression. Also consider working with a teacher in another discipline to collaborate on a text that would tie in across disciplines (e.g., science, English, etc.).

Folk Saying

See a pin, pick it up, all the day you'll have good luck. (This saying is simple, easy to write the rhythm for, and good for debating 2/4 versus 4/4. It can be done in quarters or eighths.)

Ogden Nash: 1. "The Octopus," 2. "The Eel."

Dr. Seuss (Theodor Seuss Geisel) from *One Fish, Two Fish*: It is fun to sing if you sing with a Ying.

Traditional Tongue Twisters

How much wood could a woodchuck chuck if a woodchuck could chuck wood?

One-One was a racehorse. Two-Two was one, too.
When One-One won one race, Two-Two won one, too.

Famous Sayings

After a storm comes a calm.
An apple a day keeps the doctor away.
Beauty is only skin-deep.
Do unto others as you would like them to do unto you.
Don't count your chickens before they are hatched.

Proverbs 4:18: *The path of the righteous is like the morning sun, shining ever brighter till the full light of day.*

Proverbs 6:6–8: *Go to the ant, you sluggard, consider its ways and be wise! It has no commander, no overseer or ruler, yet it stores its provisions in summer and gathers its food at harvest.*

Proverbs 15:1: *A gentle answer turns away wrath, but a harsh word stirs up anger.*

Proverbs 16:18: *Pride goes before destruction, a haughty spirit before a fall.*

Proverbs 17:14: *Starting a quarrel is like breaching a dam; so drop the matter before a dispute breaks out.*

Original Poems or Short Sayings by the Students or Teachers

Sample 1

> The band director was screaming and mad.
> He said, "Why do kids in class act so bad?
> "They have all forgot their instruments!
> "Are they lazy and ambivalent?"
> His face was bright red and his eyes full of fire,
> Until he realized he was teaching the choir!
>
> (Alexander Koops and John L. Whitener)

Sample 2

> Jumping and yelling the director came running.
> Band kids were playing and choir kids were humming.
> Strings, jazz, rock, piano, and guitar classes jammed;
> inside our ears all this music was crammed!
>
> (Alexander Koops and John L. Whitener)

Sample 3

Soft and sweet the music floated. The sound was warm . . . And gentle . . . And bloated!

(John L. Whitener)

> Horns are triumphant and violas are sad;
> Trumpets have egos, which some say is bad;
> Violins or flutes, strive for the top;
> Trombones and basses are ready to bop;
> Are ukes and guitars only a fad?
> No way, José! Let's just be glad!
>
> (Alexander Koops)

Have students in each instrument section in your ensemble write a rhyme for their instrument and then set it to music.

GO THE EXTRA MILE

Ask students to either compose a piece of their own based on a text of their own choice or to make a new arrangement of a text-based piece they like that they could perform on their own instrument or for any combination of instruments available to them in their school ensembles. Encourage exploration of diverse styles of music, including electronic music, and the use of tools like Noteflight, MuseScore, and Soundtrap®. Empower them to create for instruments/groups outside of your school ensemble as well, though encourage them to take advantage of the players around them! Let them know you will be happy to have the ensemble try out their music, anonymously if so desired, to help them develop skills to support their creativity and musical development.

NOTES

1. J. K. Rowling, *Harry Potter and the Philosopher's Stone* (London: Bloomsbury Publishing, 1997), 95.

2. Stephen Sondheim, "Stephen Sondheim Quotes," BrainyQuote, accessed December 13, 2019, https://www.brainyquote.com/quotes/stephen_sondheim_331433.

Chapter Eight

Harmony

Music is the social act of communication among people, a gesture of friendship, the strongest there is.

—Malcolm Arnold[1]

I was in a choir as a kid. It was from those early days that my outlook on harmonies and arrangements were nurtured. I always took that with me, even on the earliest Bad Religion record, which strangely was only about six years after that.

—Greg Graffin[2]

TEACHER GUIDE: LESSON 8. HARMONY

After completing this lesson, your students will be able to . . .

Define *harmony, major, minor, cluster, tension,* and *resolution*.
Create and perform a musical composition based on three or more types of harmonies.

Vocabulary Words

HARMONY: A combination of *two* or more musical tones performed at the same time, which produces a chord.
MAJOR CHORD: Three notes with the *intervals* major third plus minor third. Can be made with the first, third, and fifth notes of a major scale.

100 Chapter Eight

MINOR CHORD: Three notes with the intervals *minor* third plus major third. Can be made with the first, third, and fifth notes of a minor scale.

CLUSTER CHORD: Two or more notes in a "cluster" such as a major *second* plus a major second, or a minor second plus a minor second.

TENSION/CONFLICT: When there is rhythmic *fighting*, harmonic dissonance, and/or melodic intensity.

RESOLUTION/RELEASE: When a musical phrase feels like it has come to an *end*; when a dissonance moves to a *consonance*; when a rhythm comes to a rest or a steady place of repose.

REPOSE: *Rest* or calm; relaxed; temporary break from excitement or activity.

Lesson Activities

*See also Teacher Guide: Lesson 8. Harmony: Supplemental Materials at the end of the chapter for suggestions.

PLAY a major scale as a warmup activity for this lesson.

DISCUSS the vocabulary words and have students fill in the blanks for the definitions on their student worksheet.

(Students should have a transposed handout in B-flat for band or D major for orchestra.)

Band Sample

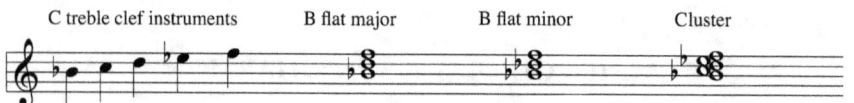

Orchestra Sample

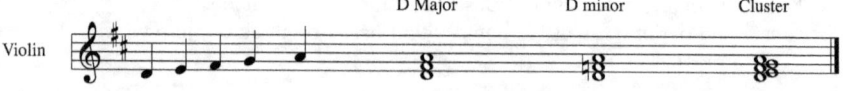

PLAY the first five notes of the scale, and then the notes of the major chord (Band: B-flat, D, F; Orchestra D, F-sharp, A). (Consider assigning players to play certain notes—for example, violins all play the top note, violas the middle note, celli/bass the bass note.) What character does it have? (Answer: happy; nice.) Remember this is a MAJOR chord.

ASK students, "How can we change the major chord into a minor chord?" (Hopefully a student will answer. If not, simply teach them how.) For a

MINOR chord, we need to lower the middle note of a major chord a half step. ASK, "What character does this minor chord have?" (Answer: sad, thoughtful, melancholy, in general.)

PLAY the cluster chord. Give students the option to randomly pick a favorite note, or play the example from the handout. ASK students, "What character does the cluster chord have?" (Answer: tense, angry if played loudly; unsettling, scary, or just colorful if played softly.)

Study TENSION and REPOSE/RESOLUTION with harmony.

PREPARE: Write in large letters on the board: MAJOR, MINOR, CLUSTER, SILENCE.

PRACTICE: Have the students play each chord as you point to it. ASK them to listen to themselves and think about the character of the harmony.

PERFORM/IMPROVISE: Have a student conductor come up and point to each group/chord in different orders, switching at will. Have the ensemble play whatever chord the student conductor points to, for as long as the conductor is pointing to that chord! Encourage the student to use silence as well! The conductor can add rhythm by simply beating his or her arm and have the ensemble re-attack the chord each time the conductors arm goes up and down, creating pulse and rhythm. Have fun with this!

ASK the students, "Which chord has the most tension?" (Answer: cluster.) "Which word on the board represents resolution or release?" (Answer: could be major, minor, or silence.)

ASK the students, "Do we have tension and repose in our lives? We can use music to express our emotions, including tension, and release from that tension. How is that expressed in music?" (See *Sample Demonstration of Tension*.) This might be a good place to use the analogy from a movie, such as *Harry Potter and the Order of the Phoenix*.

Ask for two student volunteers who are good at speaking and acting to come up and perform the following sample skits.

Sample Demonstration of Tension

Dialogue 1: Between a Child (Student A) and a Parent (Student B)

Student A. "I'm home from school."

Student B. "Welcome home! How was your day?"

Student A. "Fine."

Student B. "Did you learn anything?"

Student A. "Well, I learned that music composing is basically when you take sounds and silence and organize them."

Student B. "Well, that is exactly right; you must have a good music teacher."

Student A. "Yea, my music teacher is pretty cool: not every music teacher includes composing in their music classes."

ASK the students, "Was there any tension or repose in this dialogue/skit?" (Answer: Not much tension; more repose.)

Dialogue 2: Tension and Repose

(Student A acts as a student; Student B acts as the parent)

Student A. "Dad/Mom, can I get an iPhone?"

Student B. (soft, calm) *"No."*

Student A. "Please!"

Student B. (a little louder) *"No, I said no!"*

Student A. "All my friends have one!"

Student B. (loud commanding voice) *"No, you can't have an iPhone!"*

Student A. (shout): "Ahhh!!!!!!!"

Student B. (shout): *"Go to your room!"*

(*Dramatic pause/silence. Try to look sad.*)

Student A. (calm) "Sorry for shouting."

Student B. (calm, but reassuring) "*I forgive you.*"

DISCUSS with the students: "Was there tension? Was there repose? Was there resolution? What is tension? Is tension important in music? What is release/resolution in music? What is repose? Could the harmonies we practiced be used in a creative way to catch the spirit of this skit?"

COMPOSE: To connect the idea of tension and release in the skit about the iPhone above, have the students all participate in the following skit.

Student Handout for Dialogue Assignment—Sample Skit

Dialogue	Harmony	Dynamic	Text	Tension?	Optional: Choose Timbre
A	Major	*p*	Hello, would you like some chocolate?	Repose	Right half of the ensemble OR Soli, 3 clarinets or violins

Dialogue	Harmony	Dynamic	Text	Tension?	*Optional:* Choose Timbre
B	Major	*p*	No.	Repose	Left half of the ensemble OR Soli, 3 trumpets or violas
A	Minor	*mf*	Please.	Medium	Right half of the ensemble OR All woodwinds, or violins and violas
B	Cluster	*f*	NO!	Lots!	Left half the ensemble OR All brass or low strings
A	Minor	*p*	But,	Little	Right half of the ensemble OR 3 soli clarinets or violins
B	Cluster	*fff*	NO!!	Lots	Left half of the ensemble OR All brass and percussion or celli/bass
End	None	Silence	None	Release!	None OR Everyone take a deep breath together.

Begin by having the whole ensemble READ the skit out loud with words, as you cue them.

Part A will be performed by one half of the ensemble (right side of the group). Part B will be performed by the other half of the ensemble (left side).

Next, have the whole ensemble practice playing parts. Each part needs to be able to play major, minor, and cluster chords. Practice having EVERYONE play major, minor, and cluster chords. Be sure that each half of the room has enough students assigned to each member of the chord to produce a balanced sound.

Either CONDUCT the ensemble yourself or have student volunteers conduct. This exercise could also be done with multiple conductors: one conductor could stand in front of group A, the other in front of group B. The ensemble will play on cue from their conductor. Note that the final column gives the option to try out different timbres. If there is time, this option can be explored further. For the rhythm, just give a directed cue for each note, as suggested in the figure below.

Arrows Showing Conductor Cues for Dialogue Line

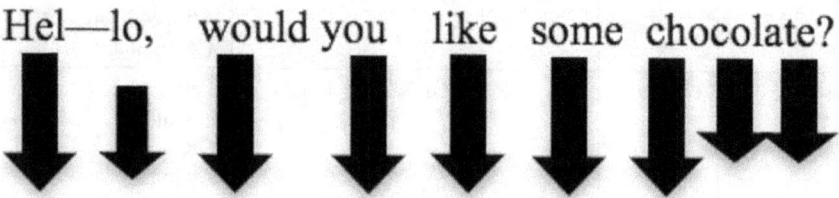

COMPOSE: Have students create their own dialogue/skit music composition in class or as homework. A chart to guide their work is included in the student worksheet.

STUDENT WORKSHEET: LESSON 8.
HARMONY—ORCHESTRA VERSION

Name: _____ Date: _____

Vocabulary

Harmony: A combination of _____ or more musical tones performed at the same time to produce chords.

Major chord: Three notes with the intervals _____ third plus minor third.

Minor chord: Three notes with the intervals _____ third plus major third.

Cluster chord: Two or more notes in a "cluster" such as a major _____ plus a major second.

Tension: When there is rhythmic _____, harmonic complexity (dissonance), and/or melodic intensity.

Resolution/Release: When a musical phrase feels like it has come to an _____; when a dissonance moves to a _____; when a rhythm comes to a rest or a steady place of repose.

Repose: _____ or calm; relaxed; temporary rest from excitement or activity.

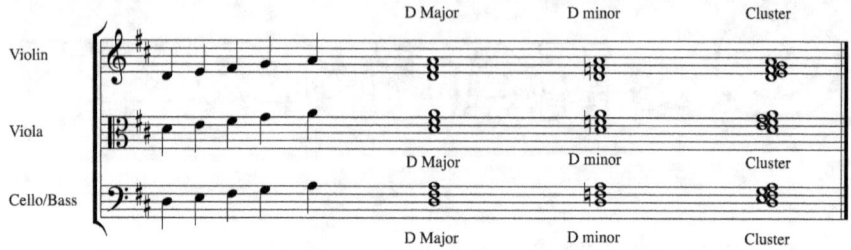

[Only this page authorized for duplication.]

Name: _____ Date: _____

Act out dialogue 1 between a parent and child and then discuss with your classmates whether there was tension in the dialogue, and if so, where it had the most tension and where it had the least tension.

Dialogue 1: Between a Child (Student A) and a Parent (Student B)

Student A. "I'm home from school."

Student B. "Welcome home! How was your day?"

Student A. "Fine."

Student B. "Did you learn anything?"

Student A. "Well, I learned that music composing is basically when you take sounds and silence and organize them."

Student B. "Well, that is exactly right; you must have a good music teacher."

Student A. "Yea, my music teacher is pretty cool: not every music teacher includes composing in their music classes."

Act out dialogue 2 between a parent and child and then discuss with your classmates whether there was tension in the dialogue, and if so, where it had the most tension and where it had the least tension.

Dialogue 2: Tension and Repose

(Student A acts as a student; Student B acts as the parent)

Student A. "Dad/Mom, can I get an iPhone?"

Student B. (soft, calm) *"No."*

Student A. "Please!"

Student B. (a little louder) *"No, I said no!"*

Student A. "All my friends have one!"

Student B. (loud commanding voice) *"No, you can't have an iPhone!"*

Student A. (shout): "Ahhh!!!!!!!"

Student B. (shout): *"Go to your room!"*

(*Dramatic pause/silence. Try to look sad.*)

Student A. (calm) "Sorry for shouting."

Student B. (calm, but reassuring) *"I forgive you."*

Compose your own dialogue and assign harmony and dynamics to it.

Student Handout for Dialogue Assignment — Sample Skit

Name: _____   Date: _____

Student Handout for Dialogue Assignment—Sample Skit

Dialogue	Harmony	Dynamic	Text	Tension?	Optional: Choose Timbre
A	Major	*p*	Hello, would you like some chocolate?	Repose	Right half of the ensemble OR Soli, 3 clarinets or violins
B	Major	*p*	No.	Repose	Left half of the ensemble OR Soli, 3 trumpets or violas
A	Minor	*mf*	Please.	Medium	Right half of the ensemble OR All woodwinds, or violins and violas
B	Cluster	*f*	NO!	Lots!	Left half the ensemble OR All brass or low strings
A	Minor	*p*	But,	Little	Right half of the ensemble OR 3 soli clarinets or violins
B	Cluster	*fff*	NO!!	Lots	Left half of the ensemble OR All brass and percussion or celli/bass
End	None	Silence	None	Release!	None OR Everyone take a deep breath together.

Blank Dialogue Chart

Dialogue Part	Harmony PICK: Major Minor Cluster	Dynamic PICK: f mf p	Tension PICK: Tension or Repose	Write text and notes about character/explanations Optional: Notate rhythm Optional: Decide timbre
A				
B				
A				
B				
A				
B				

STUDENT WORKSHEET:
LESSON 8. HARMONY—BAND VERSION

Name: _____   Date: _____

Vocabulary

Harmony: A combination of _____ or more musical tones performed at the same time to produce chords.

Major chord: Three notes with the intervals _____ third plus minor third.

Minor chord: Three notes with the intervals _____ third plus major third.

Cluster chord: Two or more notes in a "cluster" such as a Major _____ plus a major second.

Tension: When there is rhythmic _____, harmonic complexity (dissonance), and/or melodic intensity.

Resolution/Release: When a musical phrase feels like it has come to an _____; when a dissonance moves to a _____; when a rhythm comes to a rest or a steady place of repose.

Repose: _____ or calm; relaxed; temporary rest from excitement or activity.

Harmony

Name: _____ Date: _____

Act out dialogue 1 between a parent and child and then discuss with your classmates whether there was tension in the dialogue, and if so, where it had the most tension and where it had the least tension.

Dialogue 1: Between a Child (Student A) and a Parent (Student B)

Student A. "I'm home from school."

Student B. "Welcome home! How was your day?"

Student A. "Fine."

Student B. "Did you learn anything?"

Student B. "Well, that is exactly right; you must have a good music teacher."

Student A. *"Yea, my music teacher is pretty cool: not every music teacher includes composing in their music classes."*

Act out dialogue 2 between a parent and child and then discuss with your classmates whether there was tension in the dialogue, and if so, where it had the most tension and where it had the least tension.

Dialogue 2: Tension and Repose

(Student A acts as a student; Student B acts as the parent)

Student A. "Dad/Mom, can I get an iPhone?"

Student B. (soft, calm) *"No."*

Student A. "Please!"

Student B. (a little louder) *"No, I said no!"*

Student A. "All my friends have one!"

Student B. (loud commanding voice) *"No, you can't have an iPhone!"*

Student A. (shout): "Ahhh!!!!!!!"

Student B. (shout): *"Go to your room!"*

(*Dramatic pause/silence. Try to look sad.*)

Student A. (calm) "Sorry for shouting."

Student B. (calm, but reassuring) *"I forgive you."*

Compose your own dialogue and assign harmony and dynamics to it.

Student Handout for Dialogue Assignment—Sample Skit

Dialogue	Harmony	Dynamic	Text	Tension?	Optional: Choose Timbre
A	Major	*p*	Hello, would you like some chocolate?	Repose	Right half of the ensemble OR Soli, 3 clarinets or violins
B	Major	*p*	No.	Repose	Left half of the ensemble OR Soli, 3 trumpets or violas
A	Minor	*mf*	Please.	Medium	Right half of the ensemble OR All woodwinds, or violins and violas
B	Cluster	*f*	NO!	Lots!	Left half the ensemble OR All brass or low strings
A	Minor	*p*	But,	Little	Right half of the ensemble OR 3 soli clarinets or violins
B	Cluster	*fff*	NO!!	Lots	Left half of the ensemble OR All brass and percussion or celli/bass
End	None	Silence	None	Release!	None OR Everyone take a deep breath together.

[Only this page authorized for duplication.]

Chapter Eight

Name: _____ Date: _____

Blank Dialogue Chart

Dialogue Part	Harmony PICK: Major Minor Cluster	Dynamic PICK: f mf p	Tension PICK: Tension or Repose	Write text and notes about character/explanations Optional: Notate rhythm Optional: Decide timbre
A				
B				
A				
B				
A				
B				

TEACHER GUIDE: LESSON 8.
HARMONY: SUPPLEMENTAL MATERIALS

HARMONY RECOMMENDED LISTENING

For this lesson, any piece of music will work! Consider helping to expose your students to harmonies they have never heard in addition to appealing to their interests with music they love and are passionate about. The lesson focuses on major, minor, and cluster chords, so playing music examples of those three chords is a good starting point. Some diverse composers and styles you might consider include the following: Edgard Varèse, Olivier Messiaen, Pierre Boulez, Karlheinz Stockhausen, Steve Reich, J. S. Bach, Claude Gervaise, Giovanni Palestrina, Organum (Gregorian chant with added harmonies), pop rock, heavy metal, ska, reggae, hip hop, and world music, such as Indian tabla music, gamelan music, and Tibetan throat singing.

SAMPLE REPERTOIRE FOR HARMONY

For school band and orchestra repertoire related to harmony, as with the listening, any repertoire you have can work! Here are a few examples at various grade levels to consider.

BAND

Loest, Timothy   "Family Fugue" (Grade 1)
This gem is ideal for teaching major and minor tonality, melodic retrograde, dynamic contrast, and, of course, fugue form.

Del Borgo, Elliot   "Phantom Ship" (Grade 1)
This piece uses minor harmonies extensively and therefore is a great example to include in your composing lessons on harmony.

Broege, Timothy   "Headless Horseman" (Grade 2)
This piece uses dissonant cluster chords at the beginning as well as quartal harmony in the middle, in addition to a jumpy, atonal main melody. This is the type of music that is great for teaching composition because it has so many creative features packed in a top-notch, two-minute, middle school–level piece: great use of harmony, articulation, range, form, texture, and timbre.

Berk, Stacey   "Phrygian Festival Overture" (Grade 3)
In this piece, Berk selected the pitch motive D-E-C-A (to refer to the Greek word for *ten*). She explains this motive is interwoven melodically and harmonically into several sections of the work. The main scalar pattern used within the work is that of the Phrygian scale (for example, EFGABCD). This offers an exciting opportunity to discuss vertical and melodic harmonic implications in music and how composers can use scales and modes to influence their harmonic language.

Cuong, Viet   "Diamond Tide" (Grade 3)
This piece explores unique chords and harmonies and includes pitch bending in the percussion section with wine glasses as well as the trombones slowing glissing between notes. Cuong's creative approach to harmony offers your students a great opportunity for discussion and contrast-comparison to other works.

Connor, Bill   *Tails aus dem Vood Viennoise* (Grade 4–5, though there are "ripieno" parts for some instruments that are easier, Grade 3–level parts, if you have a large mixed ensemble)
This piece has major, minor, diminished, and cluster chords, as well as aleatoric sections. Because Connor is inspired partly by Mahler, you will find harmonies that are reminiscent of the late Romantic era as well as contemporary approaches. One unique feature is the use of "whirlies," which are pitched tubes that can be swung around the performer's head to create specific pitches.

ORCHESTRA

Wagner, Douglas (arranger)   "A (Very) Short History of Music" (Grade 1)
This fun piece is great for discussing harmony with young players because it represents seven different eras of music: Medieval (Gregorian chant: *Dies Irae*), Renaissance (Byrd: *The Bells*), Baroque (Vivaldi: *Autumn*), classical (Haydn: *Surprise Symphony*), Romantic (Beethoven: *Ode to Joy*), Impressionist (Satie: *Gymnopedie*), and Modern (Stravinsky: *Firebird*).

Bernofsky, Lauren   "Twilight Reverie" (Grade 1.5)

Although this piece is only a grade 1.5, composer Lauren Bernofsky explains in the notes in her score to this work that her aim was to write a serious musical piece with colorful harmonies, deep emotions, and thematic development. This piece offers clear major and minor chord examples that can be used as models or demonstrations for a student composition lesson.

Adler, Samuel   "A Little Bit of . . . Space . . . Time" (Grade 2)

This piece explores contemporary harmonies that include dissonance and is a great example to compare to other pieces when studying harmony.

Bernofsky, Lauren   "Postcard from Mars" (Grade 2.5)

This piece contains all the notes from traditional minor and major scales, but with interesting combinations—the melodic and harmonic gestures are, well, "out of this world!" This provides a perfect opportunity to connect to a creative and inspiring composing lesson.

Ellisor, Conni   "Rousing Rip Van Winkle" (Grade 3)

This creative work features use of a drone bass note as well as traditional major and minor chords.

Husa, Karel   *Vier kleine Stucke—Four Small Pieces* (Grade 3)

This piece provides a great opportunity for students to study a significant twentieth-century composer and learn how contemporary harmonies can be mixed with traditional ones in creative and moving ways.

Mitchell, Darren   "Changes in Time" (Grade 4)

This piece includes an ostinato as well as cluster chords and mixed meters, but still uses traditional major and minor chords for its basic harmonic language.

Brown, Earle   "Modules I and II" (approximately Grade 4+)

This piece is not technically that difficult, though it has some extreme ranges (whole notes), but musically it is challenging and involves a contemporary score that uses interesting creative dissonant chords, *and* two conductors. Brown explains,

> The work is scored for one large orchestra under the direction of two conductors. I consider it to be a single orchestral event made up of two simultaneous planes of sonic activity. All of the sounds are composed in each score but the two conductors may superimpose the sounds and modify their durations and loudness in spontaneous relation to one another during performance. It is an immediate collaborative activity resulting in different formal and poetic configurations in each performance, while the basic character of the work is maintained.[1]

NOTE

1. Earl Brown, "Module II," Earl Brown, Composer, accessed December 17, 2019, http://www.earle-brown.org/works/view/53.

Lesson Activities

When introducing chords at the beginning of the lesson, you may have the students consider if there is a way to make a major or minor or cluster chord sound tenser or more restful.

1. Explore with the students: try playing triple forte (*fff*) with very fast rhythm and note how it can feel tenser, even on a major chord, while mezzo piano (*mp*) on a cluster chord for the duration of a whole note is more relaxing. Experiment by playing eight eighth notes very fast, high, and loud on a major chord, followed by one whole note, low pitched, mezzo piano (*mp*) on a cluster chord.
2. Help students see that major, minor, and cluster chords can be combined with other expressive elements of music (e.g., tempo, dynamics, articulations) to change the feeling of the musical composition.
3. Consider getting into the theory side of the lesson and explain that a major chord has a major third at the bottom, and a minor chord has a minor third at the bottom. That is what makes them major or minor. Discuss intervals, consonance and dissonance, and scales. For advanced students, add inversions and modes.
4. Compose: Take an original student melody from the previous lesson on melody, or a melody from a piece in your ensemble repertoire, and add harmony to the melody. Experiment with major, minor, or cluster chords.
5. Compose: Take a set harmony that is chosen by the class with a combination of major, minor, and cluster chords, and then create a melody to go on top of the set harmony.

GO THE EXTRA MILE

An introduction to first species counterpoint could be included or an explanation of standard chord progressions like I-IV-V-I. Consider a card game like *IV-V-I: The Harmony Card Game* or create your own harmony-inspired game, such as having the ensemble play a unison melody while one or two volunteers improvise harmony bass lines or melodies.

NOTES

1. Malcolm Arnold, "Malcolm Arnold Quotes," BrainyQuote, accessed December 14, 2019, https://www.brainyquote.com/quotes/malcolm_arnold_197621.

2. Greg Graffin, "Greg Graffin Quotes," BrainyQuote, accessed December 15, 2019, https://www.brainyquote.com/quotes/greg_graffin_586557.

Chapter Nine

Form

Without craftsmanship, inspiration is a mere reed shaken in the wind.

—Johannes Brahms[1]

"Simplicity in art is everything"; when "form is intricate, contorted and difficult, communication fails, and communication is the aim of art."

—Verdi, in conversation, from notes kept by musicologist Arnaldo Bonaventura[2]

It is conceivable that what is unified form to the author or composer may of necessity be formless to his audience.

—Charles Ives[3]

TEACHER GUIDE: LESSON 9. FORM

After completing this lesson, you will be able to . . .

Define *form*, *unity*, and *contrast*.
Create and perform a composition using ABA form, showing and understanding unity and variety.

Vocabulary Words

FORM: The structure or architecture of a musical composition, such as ABA (ternary), sonata form, theme and variations, or rondo form (in other words, how a piece is *organized*).

UNITY: The concept of several *similar* ideas forming a complete and pleasing *whole*. A piece of music is unified when there are elements that *tie* it together, such as rhythm, melody, or harmony that are similar.

CONTRAST/VARIETY: The concept of being noticeably *different* from something else. In music, two or more differing ideas provide contrast and interest. Contrast can be achieved in many ways, including melody, rhythm, harmony, timbre, and range.

Composers seek to balance the elements of *unity* and *contrast* in a musical composition.

Lesson Activities

See also Teacher Guide: Lesson 9. Form: Supplemental Materials at the end of the chapter for suggestions.

PLAY a piece with ABA form. Sample repertoire is listed in the supplemental materials at the end of this chapter. After playing through an entire work, play just the opening phrase of the A theme one more time. ASK students to identify where they hear that opening music material come back later in the piece.

REFLECT on the music and help students discover the major ABA sections. Have them use pencils and label the A and B themes in their music. Try to point out something that *unifies* and ties the composition together: maybe the harmony starting and ending in the same key, or a melodic or rhythmic motive, or an ostinato. Also point out how the B section provides *contrast* either through a change of harmony, tempo, or melody.

ASK, "Who can explain or define *form* for the class? Does an essay you write in English class have form?" A poem? A painting? Architecture?

Have students *fill in* the missing blanks on their student worksheet during this discussion.

DEFINE *form* as the structure or architecture of a musical composition, such as ABA, sonata form, theme and variations, or rondo form (in other words, how a piece is organized).

EXPLAIN: Musical material that is repeated (e.g., rhythm, melodic ideas, chords, instruments, etc.) allows the listener to remember these musical ideas and look forward to hearing them again. It gives *unity* to a composition.

Ask, "What is *unity*?" DEFINE unity as the concept of several similar ideas that form a complete and pleasing *whole*. A piece of music is unified when there are similar elements that *tie* it together, such as rhythmic, melodic, or harmonic ideas that are repeated in the composition. As a listener, we expect to hear certain things based on what we have heard before (such as rhythms, melodies, harmonies, colors). We also don't want to hear the same thing too many times, or the piece becomes boring and repetitious!

What is *contrast* (or variety)? DEFINE contrast as the concept of something being noticeably *different* from something else. In music, two or more differing ideas provide contrast and interest. Contrast can be achieved in many ways, including in the melody, rhythm, harmony, timbre, and range that are used in a composition.

Sometimes a composer will surprise us with a totally new sound or musical idea! This provides contrast in a musical composition. However, the composer should also reward the listener's expectations by repeating some musical ideas so the listener doesn't get frustrated by constantly hearing new material and never hearing any familiar musical ideas. Similar or repeated ideas provide unity, different and new ideas provide contrast, and both should be balanced within the song, symphony, or composition.

One of the most basic forms in music is to present one idea (let's call it "A"), then present a different, contrasting idea (called "B"), and then go back and play the first idea ("A") one more time. This is like a musical story with a beginning, middle, and end. Does anyone know what this form is called? In music, we usually call it ABA or ternary (three-part) form.

IMAGINE an ABA composition with the students. Have them vote on what emotion and what key the A section should be in (e.g., happy: D major or B flat major). Next have them suggest what a CONTRASTING emotion and key would be (e.g., sad: B minor or G minor). Make sure to ask how the piece should end (e.g., return of A, happy: D major)! Relate the major and minor ideas back to the previous lesson on harmony.

COMPOSE! Either take the above "imaginary" composition and bring it to life, using tools from lessons 1–8, or have students pick specific musical ideas from lessons 1–8 and incorporate them into an ABA composition. Think about what your favorite or most musical and meaningful lessons were and pick ideas from those. This can be done as a class, in small groups, or individually. Have students fill their ideas in on the student worksheet ABA form chart.

If doing the project as a large ensemble, consider drawing the following blank form chart on the board. Also consider having a computer projection

SAMPLE COMPOSITION

The following composition works, but try to take your students' ideas instead of this one!

Pretend we are taking a special trip to the North Pole. First, we need to compose some music to represent the weather here at home (A section), then some music to represent the North Pole (B section). Then we will return to our weather here at home (A section).

A: Home: sunny weather, happy; soundscape with clapping and laughing as an introduction; maybe some imitation of waves crashing on the shore; major chord drone. Choose a melody from the previous lessons or create a new one. Have the melody played as a solo and then repeated with a larger group. Use an ostinato to accompany instead of a drone or in addition to the drone. Try to depict musically your weather at home.

B: The North Pole: cold, quiet, windy, dark. Use the same ostinato from the A section to provide unity, but play very soft, minor or cluster chords. Consider the timbre and range. Possibly use another contrasting melody, or no melody at all, and just a pulsating minor chord or cluster chord or soundscape.

A: Then repeat A again, but consider some slight variation of the material.

screen available, putting student suggestions right into a notation program on your computer and getting immediate feedback from your students. If you assign this composition as an individual or small group project, a sample assessment rubric is provided here.

Blank Form Chart: ABA Composition

	Part A
Description of idea	
Dynamic	
Rhythm	
Texture (thick, thin, homo/poly/ monophony)	
Instrumentation (or timbre)	
Harmony and/or accompaniment	

	Part B
Description of idea	
Dynamic	
Rhythm	
Texture (thick, thin, homo/poly/ monophony)	
Instrumentation (or timbre)	
Harmony and/or accompaniment	

	(Part A repeated—note any changes?)
Description of idea	
Dynamic	
Rhythm	
Texture (thick, thin, homo/poly/ monophony)	
Instrumentation (or timbre)	
Harmony and/or accompaniment	

Sample Assessment Rubric for ABA Composition

Adapt as needed to emphasize the important concepts in your particular situation.

Consider:	0 points	1 point	2 points	3 points
Description of idea	None labeled	Vague	Clear	Inspiring
Dynamic	None labeled	One only	2 dynamics	3 or more used; creative dynamics
Rhythm	None labeled	Has some rhythm notated, but not quite accurate	Interesting rhythm, and gets the point across; may have made one rhythmic mistake	Inspired rhythm, accurately notated
Texture (thick, thin, homo/poly/ monophony)	None labeled	Somehow described	Clearly described and varied	Clearly described, varied, and shows creative thought
Instrumentation (or timbre)	None labeled	Somehow described	Clearly described	Clearly described and is creative
Harmony	None	At least one chord or accompaniment idea included, but not necessarily in a meaningful way	At least one chord or accompaniment idea included; fits fine with the composition	Creatively incorporated in a meaningful way; adds a lot to the composition
Form	Does not have any evidence of ABA form	Has a suggestion of ABA form, but is missing a significant aspect	Has a great start on ABA form, but could use some more clarity or contrast for one section such as the A or B section	Creative ABA form
Consider:				
Overall Creativity	Simple and short— followed the directions but did not show evidence of creativity.	One or more creative ideas, but consider exploring more!	Good creative approach! Shows signs of exploring and trying new ideas out.	Multiple points in the music show evidence of creativity and originality in the ideas.

STUDENT WORKSHEET: LESSON 9. FORM

Name: _____ Date: _____

Vocabulary

Form: The structure or architecture of a musical composition, such as _____ (ternary), sonata form, theme and variations, or rondo form (in other words, how a piece is _____).

Unity: The concept of several similar ideas forming a complete and pleasing _____. A piece of music is unified when there are elements that _____ it together, such as rhythm, melody, or harmony.

Contrast/Variety: The concept of being noticeably _____ from something else. In music two or more differing ideas provide contrast/variety and interest. Contrast can be achieved in many ways, including melody, rhythm, harmony, timbre, and range.

Lesson Activities

Write down your idea for an ABA composition that represents two contrasting ideas taken from previous lessons. Use either traditional notation on staff paper, the form chart here, or both, as directed by your teacher.

Blank Form Chart: ABA Composition

	Part A
Description of idea	
Dynamic	
Rhythm	
Texture (thick, thin, homo/poly/ monophony)	
Instrumentation (or timbre)	
Harmony and/or accompaniment	

	Part B
Description of idea	
Dynamic	
Rhythm	
Texture (thick, thin, homo/poly/ monophony)	
Instrumentation (or timbre)	
Harmony and/or accompaniment	

	(Part A repeated—note any changes?)
Description of idea	
Dynamic	
Rhythm	
Texture (thick, thin, homo/poly/ monophony)	
Instrumentation (or timbre)	
Harmony and/or accompaniment	

Name: _____ Date: _____

ABA Composition

[Only this page authorized for duplication.]

TEACHER GUIDE: LESSON 9.
FORM: SUPPLEMENTAL MATERIALS

FORM RECOMMENDED LISTENING

Every great piece of music of any style has form of some sort or another, so pick one of your favorites and share the form with your students. Many of J. S. Bach's works, such as the *Cello Suites*, have short movements that are in ABA form. All minuet and trios from the classical repertoire are ternary forms, such as Ludwig van Beethoven's Piano Sonata in B-flat. op. 22, Menuetto. Robert Schumann's *Album for the Young* (piano repertoire) has many short ternary forms that are good examples (e.g., Volksliedchen, Wilder Reiter, Knecht Ruprecht).

Teaching Music through Performance in Band, volume 3, has a chapter that specifically deals with form in music and lists band tunes that are in specific forms, including ternary. A classic band example is Ralph Vaughan Williams's "Flourish for Wind Band"—in ternary form. Orchestra music is well-documented and you can find examples from your undergraduate music history classes such as the theme from Johannes Brahms's *Variations on a Theme of Haydn*, or any minuet and trio from a classical symphony or string quartet. A great example to introduce rondo form, if you expand past ABA and go to ABACADA, is Zoltán Kodály's "Viennese Musical Clock."

CONNECTION TO PUBLISHED REPERTOIRE FOR FORM

Just as in the suggestions for listening examples, any one of your ensemble's regular repertoire pieces will work to demonstrate form. Consider using famous songs like Beethoven's "Ode to Joy" to reinforce the concept of ABA: note how Beethoven creates phrases that are AA'BA, and challenge students to do the same. Below are some specific examples in ternary form to start you off, but be sure and help the students learn the form of every piece you perform!

BAND EXAMPLES

Daehn, Larry   "Song for Friends" (Grade 1)

This beautiful piece is great for teaching ABA form as well as melody, accompaniment, musical phrases, slurs, and dynamics.

Ticheli, Frank   "December Snow" (Grade 1)

This piece has a clear ABA Coda form, and uses 3/4 time in part A and 4/4 time in part B, offering a perfect teaching opportunity for form as well as for unity and contrast. Ticheli also uses a canon at the end, offering the chance to review homophonic and polyphonic textures from the previous texture composition lesson.

Margolis, Bob   "Fanfare" from *Fanfare Ode and Festival* (Grade 2)
                         (based on Gervaise)

The form follows a clear ABA format, featuring interesting harmony, timbre, and texture changes. The A section starts with brass and percussion in B-flat major with four-part texture, followed by the B section in a Dorian mode with the woodwinds joining in a contrasting theme with two-part texture. The final A returns with the whole ensemble back in major mode.

Nishimura, Cait   "Chasing Sunlight" (Grade 2)

This delightful piece can be analyzed a few different ways, but can be seen as an opening section A, followed by a B section, and then ending with a final C section that uses both the A and B section materials. It is a great piece with lots of composition lessons that can be learned from it, including texture, timbre, harmony, ostinato, as well as form.

Erickson, Frank   "Air for Band" (Grade 2+)

This classic band work is most often analyzed as a ternary form but actually offers a great opportunity to see how a creative composer can work with form. The A section is like the first verse of a song, followed by the B section (m. 17), which acts like a chorus. The A material returns in m. 28, and just when the piece could end, Erickson brings out the B section material as a coda but develops it a bit at m. 36, leading to the end of the work. It also has a wonderful mix of major and minor harmonies, sweet suspensions, and an inspiring ending in C major, after spending the majority of the work in C minor and E-flat major.

Vaughn Williams, Ralph   "Flourish for Wind Band" (Grade 3)

Every grade 3 band should play this work by one of the most famous British composers of the twentieth century. It has a clear ABA form as well as creative imitation, seen and heard with polyphonic texture in the A sections and more homophonic texture in the B section.

Archer, Kimberly   "Beacon" (Grade 3)

This piece is loosely in three sections. Young composers need to see creative examples of how to connect and transition between different sections of music. This piece sets apart sections with tempo changes as well as harmony, texture, and timbre changes.

ORCHESTRA

Bernofsky, Lauren   "Dinosaur Damage" (Grade 1)

This ternary-form piece has a clear contrasting B section and is fun to play. Bernofsky starts in E minor, which offers a great opportunity to connect with the previous harmony lesson. The B section features the low strings while the violins stay on an E, with various rhythms, allowing you to introduce the compositional concept of a drone in the upper voices!

Day, Susan   "Eagle's Pride" (Grade 1.5)

Composer Susan Day uses da capo form in this high-energy piece. As students learn about ABA form, they can see that, on a da capo, they are going back to play the A section again!

Del Borgo, Elliot   "Dance Scenario" (Grade 2)

This piece starts out energetically, but then switches to a cantabile section in the middle before returning for an all-out ending. A great example for teaching ternary form as well as the concepts of unity and contrast.

Fin, Loreta   Tarantella (Grade 3)

This string work is written in the Southern Italian dance style with compound duple meter and minor tonality. The C major middle section makes the piece ideal to teach relative keys, as well as ternary form. The offbeat accompaniment is essential, and can be played on a piano, accordion, or keyboard with accordion voice.

Beethoven, Ludwig van   "Adagio Cantabile" (from *"Pathetique" Sonata*),
                                     arr. Carrie Lane Gruselle (Grade 3)

This famous piece allows many teaching opportunities relating to composition, including an ABA form with a short coda at the end. Every student deserves a chance to learn from Beethoven!

Wada, Naoya   "Remembrance" (Grade 3)

This beautiful string orchestra piece is also arranged for band. Japanese composer Naoya Wada loosely follows a three-part form, starting in 4/4, moving to 3/4 in the middle section, and briefly bringing back the opening theme at the conclusion of the piece. While the piece is not a clear ternary form, there are clear, contrasting sections and creative developments of themes that provide an interesting study in form. Composition lessons on this piece may also focus on use of articulation, dynamics, tempo changes, texture, and harmony. Nice solos for violin and cello appear in the middle, featuring thin textures contrasting with tutti passages.

Lesson Activities

Consider showing a classical painting, such as *Madonna di San Sisto* by Raphael Sanzio or *Coronation of the Virgin* by Diego Velazquez, and discuss its form, showing off the balance. Compare that to the balance in a piece of music with ternary form. Present a building or sculpture and describe its form. See how forms can be clear, but also may be flexible, creative, and blurred. Study the form of a poem or lyrics of a song (alternating verse and chorus, and possibly adding a bridge).

Discuss the importance of repetition and contrast in relation to listeners' understanding and enjoyment of a new composition. Levitin discusses this concept in his book *This Is Your Brain on Music* (also quoted at the beginning of this book in chapter 1).

Music is organized sound, but the organization has to involve some element of the unexpected or it is emotionally flat and robotic. . . . Composers imbue music with emotion by knowing what our expectations are and then very deliberately controlling when those expectations will be met, and when they won't. The thrills, chills, and tears we experience from music are the result of having our expectations artfully manipulated by a skilled composer and the musicians who interpret that music.[4]

Additional Sample Compositions

ABA Composition #1

A theme: FAST-EXCITED: Trombones come in with the coffee grinder / car rev sound, then slowly the whole ensemble gradually joins in the rhythmic, pulsing car rev sound, as best they can imitate it on their instruments (e.g., the bass drum can even roll with a crescendo and diminuendo). This builds to a grand climax with a crash cymbal on cue (chapter 3, on rhythm).

B theme: SLOW-MELANCHOLY: Let's create a sad, contrasting section by using ideas from the soundscape lesson plan. Some ensemble members could moan, while others play minor chords and cluster chords on half or whole notes, alternating these ideas. GO SLOWLY to catch the spirit of melancholy—and play softly! Students should be expressive, adding crescendos and diminuendos for more dramatic emotional effect.

Return of the A theme: FAST-EXCITED: Trombones again come in with the coffee grinder / car rev sound. After a bit, the remaining brass enter with half valves and all the woodwinds, imitating, building to a grand climax, with bass drum and a crash cymbal on cue.

Sample ABA Composition #2

A—Pick a rhythm from a rhythm lesson and some chords from the harmony lesson.
B—Pick a melody or two from the melody lesson and assign a timbre and texture from the texture and timbre lessons.
A'—Return to the opening section (A), but change some aspect slightly, while being sure that enough is the same that the listener will recognize it is a return of the opening material.

GO THE EXTRA MILE

Explore other forms based on repertoire you are playing and challenge students to compose their own individual compositions with a form of their own choosing. Consider expanding to a five-part rondo ABACA or a theme and variations. Consider solos, small ensembles, or full ensemble.

NOTES

1. Johannes Brahms, "Johannes Brahms Quotes," AllGreatQuotes, accessed December 16, 2019, https://www.allgreatquotes.com/quote-227006/.
2. Arnaldo Bonaventura, *Ricordi e ritratti* [Memories and Portraits], quoted in George W. Martin, *Aspects of Verdi* (New York: Limelight Editions, 1993), v.
3. R. Monelle, *The Sense of Music: Semiotic Essays* (Princeton, NJ: Princeton University Press, 2000), 219, https://ebookcentral.proquest.com.
4. Daniel J. Levitin, "Daniel J. Levitin Quotes," Notable Quotes, from *This Is Your Brain on Music*, accessed June 1, 2015, http://www.notable-quotes.com/l/levitin_daniel_j.html#p9jPObm7HqbhJRuj.99.

Chapter Ten

Final Composition

The true sign of intelligence is not knowledge but imagination.

—Albert Einstein[1]

Real art is one of the most powerful forces in the rise of mankind, and he who renders it accessible to as many people as possible is a benefactor of humanity.

—Zoltán Kodály[2]

I haven't understood a bar of music in my life, but I have felt it.

—Igor Stravinsky[3]

The musical experiences that are most memorable are the magical moments when expectation is subverted, when complacency is destroyed, and when a new world opens.

—Jonathan Kramer[4]

TEACHER GUIDE: LESSON 10. FINAL COMPOSITION

After completing this lesson, your students will be able to . . .

Define *form, rondo form, theme and variations, layering,* and *channel surfing.* Create and perform a composition using the channel surfing form and ideas from the tool bank of lessons 1–9.

Vocabulary Words

LAYERING: Combining things on *top* of one another. In music, this involves putting musical ideas on top of one another, different ideas sounding together.

CHANNEL SURFING: When watching TV, *switching* channels randomly as soon as you get tired of one channel or have seen enough to know what is going on at that channel. In music, it is kind of like switching music radio stations: as soon as you hear enough to know what is going on, you switch the channel. Some channels (musical ideas) may attract you more than others, so you may listen to them longer.

FORM: The *structure* or architecture of a musical composition, such as ABA, sonata form, theme and variations, or rondo form (in other words, how a piece is *organized*).

RONDO FORM: A form structure in music that involves a main theme (A) that alternates with *contrasting* themes (B, C, D, etc.), such as ABACA, or ABACABA.

THEME AND VARIATIONS: A main musical theme is presented, and then variations, or slight alterations of that theme, are created. The variations are all related to the main theme, through altering different aspects of its structure. Musical elements from these composition lessons—such as soundscape accompaniments, rhythm, orchestration or timbre, texture, melody, harmony, and tempo—may all be changed to create or elicit different feelings and interpretations of the original theme.

Lesson Activities

*See also Teacher Guide: Lesson 10. Final Composition: Supplemental Materials at the end of the chapter for suggestions.

REVIEW AND PLAY a selection of the previous compositions. BRIEFLY review each concept: soundscapes, timbre, rhythm from life, ostinato, melody, texture, harmony, and form.

DEFINE and explain the new vocabulary, as listed above: Layering, Channel Surfing, Form, Rondo Form, and Theme and Variations. If possible, relate your regular repertoire to these forms.

VOTE on which form the students would like to explore for the final composition, or break this lesson into multiple lessons. You could choose to do a large group composition or smaller group compositions. If there was a melody that stood out from one of the previous lessons, you might choose to use that as a rondo theme or a variation theme and develop the composition based on that. If not, the channel surfing form is a fun way to cover lots of ideas in a single compositional mix.

DISCUSS these possibilities of different forms

- Theme and variations form: Good if you have one melody that everyone likes.
- Rondo form: Fun if you have several melodies or themes you like because you can alternate a variety of themes with one that is the main theme.
- Channel surfing: This is a great way to pick a variety of favorite lessons and randomly put them back to back, switching back and forth between themes. This could be the whole ensemble playing but it also could involve solos and small groups.

COMPOSE! The grand finale! To put together the final composition, encourage students to consider all the tools they have learned.

> **SAMPLE CHANNEL SURFING COMPOSITION**
>
> 1. *Introduction*: Soundscapes
> 2. *Timbre*: A dog chasing a cat—percussion, trombones—snare drum, wood block, trombones "barking" by playing notes with glisses that sound like barks
> 3. *Rhythm from life* (woodwinds)
> 4. *Ostinato* (percussion)
> 5. *Texture*: Pick one idea from the lesson: sample. (Start monophonic, then homophonic, and then move to polyphonic. Use some of the student solos that were written.)
> 6. *Melody 1*: Pick one melody from melody lesson (brass feature).
> 7. *Melody 2*: From poem/words lesson (woodwind feature).
> 8. *Harmony* (full ensemble). See student handout; decide on a rhythm and then repeat the rhythm with pitches that are in minor, major, minor, cluster, silence, major (your choice).
> 9. Consider ending with the soundscape as a conclusion or layering several of these ideas together simultaneously:

If you choose the channel surfing composition, the conductor can help assign groups within the ensemble to perform certain "channels," or everyone can play all the channels. Favorite channels can be turned on more often, and the volume can also be adjusted. Have the band/orchestra vote on the method for how to "switch channels." Richard Meyer has one player assigned to hit a bell to signal the switching of the channels, though this could be done in any number of creative ways, including visual aids or simply watching the conductor and following the music plan.

PERFORM the final group composition, and PLAY some student works as well.

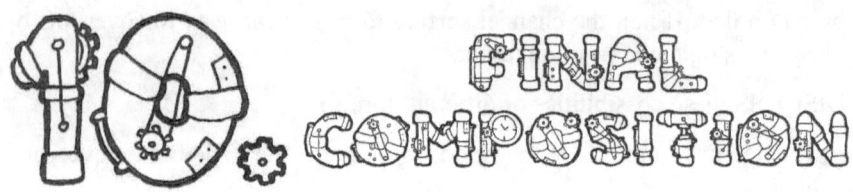

STUDENT WORKSHEET: LESSON 10.
FINAL COMPOSITION PROJECT

Name: _____ Date: _____

Vocabulary

Layering: Putting things on _____ of one another. In music, this involves putting musical ideas on top of one another, different ideas sounding together.

Channel surfing: When watching TV, _____ channels randomly as soon as you get tired of one channel or have seen enough to know what is going on at that channel. In music, it is kind of like switching music radio stations: as soon as you hear enough to know what is going on, you switch the channel. Some channels may attract you more than others, so you may listen to them longer.

Form: The _____ of a musical composition, such as ABA, sonata form, theme and variations, or rondo form (in other words, how a piece is _____).

Rondo form: A structure in music that involves a main theme that alternates with _____ themes, such as ABACA or ABACADA.

Theme and variations: A main musical theme is presented, and then variations are created, all related to the main theme, through altering different aspects of the theme. Musical elements from these composition lessons—such as soundscape accompaniments, rhythm, orchestration or _____, texture, melody, harmony, and tempo—may all be changed to offer different feelings and interpretations of the original theme.

Final Composition

Lesson Activities

Using everything you have learned about composition and any other musical skills and ideas you have, create a new composition that your section or ensemble can perform. It may need to be written on one or more pieces of paper and have enough information so that other students will be able to play the music you have created without any verbal explanation.

Here is a list of some of the composition lessons you have covered and could potentially use in your final composition:

- Soundscapes: Using nontraditional sounds in combination
- Timbre or instrumentation: Choosing which instruments or sounds to use
- Rhythm: Rhythms from life or rhythms from words/poetry
- Ostinato: A repeated musical idea or rhythm
- Texture: Thick (many instruments or ideas) or thin (just a few ideas, or solo)
    - Monophony—a single line/melody of music
    - Homophony—a single line of music with harmony or accompaniment
    - Polyphony—two or more lines/melodies of music at the same time
- Melody: Using the first five notes of a major scale
- Harmony: Major, minor, cluster chords; tension-repose
- Form: Lesson 9 uses of ABA form could be perfect for this project. Discuss the forms listed in the vocabulary section with your teacher and vote on which one would suit your class best!

Ask your teacher for extra staff paper if you need it. Label the form of your composition. You should also include dynamics, articulations, and tempo

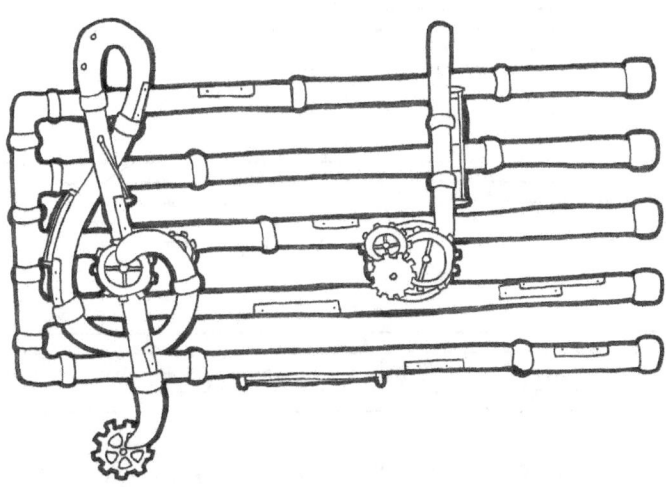

changes. You could use graphic notation or traditional notation.

With the class or with a friend(s), compose your own new piece. Organize your ideas and sounds by writing in the staff lines or using words to describe your composition.

Have fun, be creative, and do the best you can!

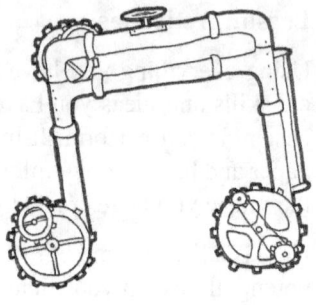

[Only this page authorized for duplication.]

TEACHER GUIDE: LESSON 10. FINAL COMPOSITION: SUPPLEMENTAL MATERIALS

FINAL COMPOSITION RECOMMENDED LISTENING

As with chapter 9, any piece can work for listening for this topic. Richard Meyer's string orchestra piece "Remote Control" (Grade 2.5) is a great example of a fun channel surfing piece using famous tunes. John Corigliano's Symphony 3 for Bands: Circus Maximus has a movement that is titled Channel Surfing (Grade 6). Pieces written with a "theme and variations" form abound, and Wolfgang Amadeus Mozart's *Ah vous dirai-je, Maman*, K. 265/300e (Twinkle, Twinkle Variations) or Charles Ives's *Variations on "America"* are both great examples to share with students. Gustav Holst's First Suite in E-flat, Movement 1: Chaconne is a great example of an eight-bar bass theme that gets repeated over and over with creative development above and below the theme. Holst's *St. Paul's Suite* for string orchestra features a repeated melody in the Finale (The Dargason), and the same tune is featured in his *Second Suite in F*, Finale (Fantasia on the Dargason). As mentioned in the previous chapter, Zoltán Kodály's "Viennese Musical Clock" from *Hary Janos Suite* (full orchestra) features a rondo form ABACADA. Other examples of rondo include Mozart's Horn Concerto 4 in E flat, and Percy Grainger's Molly on the Shore. Finally, also consider listening to march music, pop music, movie music, and world music and studying the forms of those pieces with your students.

Connection to Published Repertoire

The American Composer's Forum has commissioned many great, new works by contemporary composers representing both men and women and people of color and they include amazing lesson plans covering the National Core Arts Standards (creating, performing, responding, connecting). The curriculum with lesson plans is offered free through their programs called BandQuest and ChoralQuest on their website. All of their repertoire is highly recommended (mostly grade 2 and 3 level), but even if you don't buy one of their pieces, you can still download the curriculum packages to get sample lessons on composing, so definitely don't miss that resource. Additionally, use the Composer Diversity Database (sponsored by the Institute for Composer Diversity) to help pick band or orchestra pieces at the specific grade level you need that represent women composers and composers of color: https://www.composerdiversity.com/.

The table here has recommended pieces, but a couple composers deserve special consideration in relation to supporting creativity in your band and orchestra classes. Jodie Blackshaw has published many pieces that support creativity, including beginning band pieces through advanced band pieces. Her beginning band project piece Belah Sun Woman is a multi-movement work designed to be worked on throughout the first year and involves great musicianship lessons that include creativity for your first-year band students.

If you are an orchestra director, you might consider buying just the score and using her ideas to design your own orchestra project piece for first-year orchestra students. Blackshaw has also published *13 Moons: Composing Pieces*, and these are designed for Grades 1-, 2-, 3-, and 4-level band, so this piece can work for any grade level you teach! You could easily adapt this piece to orchestra as well. Her concept in this work is to provide the music teacher and students with building blocks for composition and enable the ensemble to creatively use the materials to build a piece in their own unique and creative way. Another example of a composing project piece is Libby Larsen's *An Introduction to the Moon* (Grades 4–5), which provides a framework with some composed music, but also gives spaces for students to pick and choose their own favorite poems about the moon and compose music to match the poems.

Sample Repertoire: Final Composition

Band Pieces		
Composer Title	Form	Grade
Ticheli, F. *Peace*	Binary form: ABA'B'	1
Blackshaw, Jodie *Belah Sun Woman*	4 movements; form based on narrative traditional folklore from Australia; designed as a project piece for beginning band to be worked on throughout the year	0.5–1.5
Blackshaw, Jodie *13 Moons: Composing Pieces*	Open—students create and organize the music themselves	1–4+
Broege, T. *The Headless Horseman*	Arc form: Intro ABCBA Coda	2
Higdon, Jennifer *Rhythm Stand*	Introduction and 5 sections ABCDE with lots of amazing and inspiring lesson plans, all prepared by the American Composers Forum / BandQuest	2–3
Blackshaw, Jodie *Letter from Sado*	Ternary form: ABA; free resources from BandQuest to help teach composition and creativity!	3
Erb, Donald *Space Music*	Ternary form: ABA; lots of contemporary techniques, atonal	3–4
Day, Kevin *Rocketship!*	Ternary form: ABA	3–4
Holst, G. *First Suite in E-flat*	Chaconne form: Movement 1: Chaconne. An 8-bar theme repeated with variations	4
Larsen, Libby *An Introduction to the Moon*	Open continuous form with an alternation of interlude music with sections for students to compose their own music to match poetry about the moon	4–5

Orchestra Pieces

Composer Title	Form	Grade
Meyer, R. *Miniature Symphony*	Symphony form: 4 movements with various forms and composition techniques including march form, ternary form, minuet and trio form, canonic techniques, and use of D.S. (Dal Segno—Go back to the sign) and D.C. (Da Capo—Go back to the top), which are often used to create ABA forms	0.5
Straub, Dorothy *Simple Square Dance*	Ternary: ABA	1
Schubert, F. Theme and Variations from the *"Trout" Quintet*, arr. A. H. Dabczynski	Theme and variations form; an important classical example of this form	1.5
Nishimura, Yukiko *Prelude to an Old Tale*	Arc form: ABCA: short introduction followed by a main theme that is repeated and developed a bit, then a short contrasting section, and then a return the main theme	2
Meyer, R. *Remote Control*	Remote control form or moment form	2.5
Johnson, Darryl *The Perfect Morning*	Continuous development: ABA'CDA"A'"A""	3
Bach, J. S. *Fugue in G Minor* (*The Little Fugue*), arr. Gerald R. Doan	Fugue	3
Atwell, Shirl Jae *Modus à 4*	Sectional form: ABCD; first 2 melodies introduced homophonic, then 2 melodies polyphonic, then all four together at the end!	3
Holst, G. *St. Paul's Suite*, Finale: The Dargason	Basso ostinato form: 8-bar melody over and over with variations (this is the same tune used in the *Second Suite in F for band*)	4

Lesson Activities

For the final composing project, if you choose the "channel surfing" concept, consider having your large ensemble broken into smaller groups that each compose a short piece, and then those pieces are placed in a certain order and could be called a "channel surfing" form. The conductor can point to each group to play their section of music in its entirety, then start pointing to random groups or even more than one group at a time, faster and faster, ending with everyone playing. An option for ending this extravaganza could be a big cymbal crash from the percussion section, or whip or bass drum. Additionally, encourage students to add physical movements to the music. The composer John Corigliano has an amazing "channel surfing" section in his wind ensemble piece *Circus Maximus* that uses smaller ensembles offstage in balconies surrounding the hall. He builds up to a climax in which all groups are playing simultaneously creating an almost unbearable, incohesive noise that slowly dissipates to a single clarinetist. He also ends his *Circus Maximus* with a blast from a shotgun.

Channel surfing form is related to *moment form*. Kramer in his book *The Time of Music* defines moment form as "a mosaic of moments," and a moment is defined as a "self-contained (quasi-)independent section, set off from other sections by discontinuities."[5] Listeners generally need a balance of repeated material and new material: if you have too much repetition of ideas your listener will get bored, but if you surprise your listener constantly without repeating anything, they will be frustrated! Help your students experiment with finding the right balance of repeated and new materials as they develop their compositions.

GO THE EXTRA MILE

Study more forms in music that relate to the repertoire you are performing such as march form, sonata form, arch form, narrative form, arch form, tone poem, song form, blues form, and so on. Assign students to compose new works in one or more of those forms. Another interesting assignment is to ask students to pick a piece of music they like (this could be any style, including hip hop, country, world music, etc.), and see if they can figure out the form of the piece and write it down.

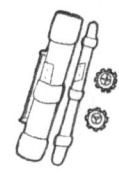

Final Composition

TEST 3: LESSONS 7–10. TEXT-BASED COMPOSING, HARMONY, FORM

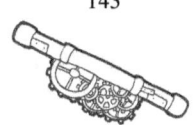

Name _____

Match the following words with their correct definition by writing the correct letter in the blank:

1. _____ Word or text painting
2. _____ Major chord
3. _____ Cluster chord
4. _____ Rhythm
5. _____ Tension
6. _____ Syllable
7. _____ Layering
8. _____ Harmony
9. _____ Form
10. _____ Minor chord
11. _____ Contrast
12. _____ Channel surfing
13. _____ Unity
14. _____ Resolution (release)

A. A pattern of beats in music
B. A part or whole of a word having one vowel sound
C. An attempt with music to represent a certain word or words in a text
D. A combination of three or more musical tones performed at the same time to produce chords
E. Three notes with the intervals major third plus minor third
F. Three notes with the intervals minor third plus major third
G. Two or more notes in a "cluster" such as major second plus major second
H. When there is rhythmic fighting, harmonic complexity (dissonance), melodic intensity
I. When a musical phrase feels like it has come to an end; when a dissonance moves to a consonance; when a rhythm comes to a rest or a steady place
J. The structure of a musical composition, such as ABA, sonata form, theme and variations, or rondo form (in other words, how a piece is organized)
K. The concept of several ideas forming a complete and pleasing whole; a piece of music is unified when there are elements that tie it together, such as rhythm, melody, or harmony
L. The concept of being noticeably different from something else
M. Putting things on top of one another; in music, this involves putting musical ideas on top of one another.
N. When watching TV, switching channels randomly as soon as you get tired of one channel or have seen enough to know what is going on at that channel

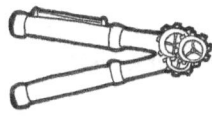

144   *Chapter Ten*

15/16. How does Mozart use text painting in the following audio example: Mozart: *Requiem in D Minor, K 626–3: Sequentia, Dies Irae*.

Circle the two correct answers: A   B   C   D

A. A minor key represents sadness and anger.
B. A major key is used to represent sadness and anger.
C. Cluster chords are used to create a hopeful, happy soundscape.
D. Sharp articulations and rhythms are used to create an angry and desperate feeling.

17–25 (8 pts. total: 4 pts. rhythm; 2 pts. bar lines; 1 pt. phrases; 1 pt. time signature)

1. Derive the rhythm from the following text.
2. Figure out the phrases, groups, or patterns of rhythm and add phrase markings.
3. Figure out the time signature based on the phrases and write the time signature at the beginning.
4. Mark where the bar lines should go and insert them based on the phrases and the time signature.

"See a pin, pick it up, all the day you'll have good luck!"

26–30. Identify the form of a piece of music from your ensemble repertoire or as assigned by your teacher and describe the character of the theme(s) (4 pts.):

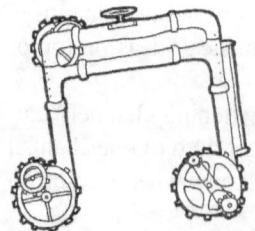

TEACHER ANSWER KEY: TEST 3. LESSONS 7–10

Name: TEACHER

Match the following words with their correct definition by writing the correct letter in the blank:

1. Word or text painting: C
2. Major chord: E
3. Cluster chord: G
4. Rhythm: A
5. Tension: H
6. Syllable: B
7. Layering: M
8. Harmony: D
9. Form: J
10. Minor chord: F
11. Contrast: L
12. Channel surfing: N
13. Unity: K
14. Resolution (release): I

A. A pattern of beats in music
B. A part or whole of a word having one vowel sound
C. An attempt with music to represent a certain word or words in a text
D. A combination of three or more musical tones performed at the same time to produce chords
E. Three notes with the intervals major third plus minor third
F. Three notes with the intervals minor third plus major third
G. Two or more notes in a "cluster" such as major second plus major second
H. When there is rhythmic fighting, harmonic complexity (dissonance), melodic intensity
I. When a musical phrase feels like it has come to an end; when a dissonance moves to a consonance; when a rhythm comes to a rest or a steady place
J. The structure of a musical composition, such as ABA, sonata form, theme and variations, or rondo form (in other words, how a piece is organized)
K. The concept of several ideas forming a complete and pleasing whole; a piece of music is unified when there are elements that tie it together, such as rhythm, melody, or harmony
L. The concept of being noticeably different from something else
M. Putting things on top of one another; in music, this involves putting musical ideas on top of one another

N. When watching TV, switching channels randomly as soon as you get tired of one channel or have seen enough to know what is going on at that channel

15/16. How does Mozart use text painting in the following audio example:

Listening: Mozart: *Requiem in D Minor, K 626–3: Sequentia, Dies Irae.*

Circle the two correct answers: A and D.

A. A minor key represents sadness and anger.

D. Sharp articulations and rhythms are used to create an angry and desperate feeling.

17–25 (8 pts. total: 4 pts. rhythm; 2 pts. bar lines; 1 pt. phrases; 1 pt. time signature)

1. Derive the rhythm from the following text.
2. Figure out the phrases, groups, or patterns of rhythm and add phrase markings.
3. Figure out the time signature based on the phrases and write the time signature at the beginning.
4. Mark where the bar lines should go and insert them based on the phrases and the time signature.

"See a pin, pick it up, all the day you'll have good luck!"

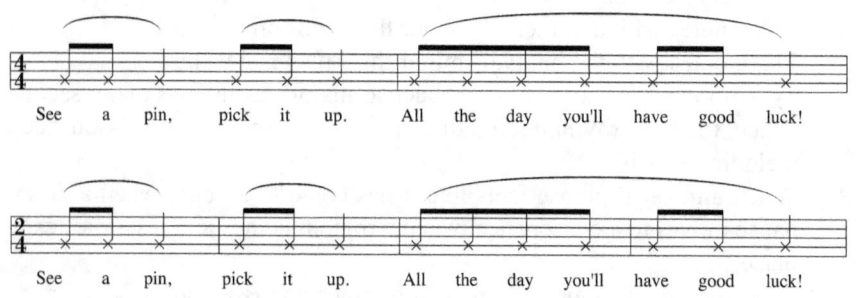

26–30. Identify the form of a piece of music from your ensemble repertoire or as assigned by your teacher and describe the character of the theme(s) (4 pts.).

NOTES

1. Albert Einstein, "Albert Einstein Quotes," BrainyQuote, accessed December 17, 2019, https://www.brainyquote.com/quotes/albert_einstein_148802.
2. Zoltan Kodaly, "Zoltan Kodaly Quotes" BrainyQuote, accessed December 17, 2019, https://www.brainyquote.com/quotes/zoltan_kodaly_205663.
3. Igor Stravinsky, "Igor Stravinsky Quotes," BrainyQuote, accessed December 17, 2019, https://www.brainyquote.com/quotes/igor_stravinsky_141127.
4. Jonathan Kramer, *The Time of Music: New Meanings, New Temporalities, New Listening Strategies* (New York: Schirmer Books; London: Collier Macmillan, 1988), 177.
5. Kramer, *The Time of Music*, 453.

Appendix 1
Dynamics and Articulations Charts

Dynamics Chart

Italian Term	English Translation
Pianissimo (*pp*)	Very soft
Piano (*p*)	Soft
Mezzo piano (*mp*)	Medium soft
Mezzo forte (*mf*)	Medium loud
Forte (*f*)	Loud
Fortissimo (*ff*)	Very loud
Crescendo	Get gradually louder
Decrescendo	Get gradually softer
Sforzando (*sfz*)	Strong, sudden accent
Subito piano (*sub. p*)	Suddenly soft
Morendo	Dying away

Articulations Chart

Italian Term	Symbol	English Translation
Accent	>	Attack note strongly
Glissando	(musical notation: Sal- mon rolls)	Continuous slide in between the notes
Legato	⌢	Very smoothly articulated, full-length, no separation
Marcato	∧	Very strong accent, slight separation between notes
Pizzicato	+	For string players, pluck the strings instead of bowing
Staccato	•	Very short, detached
Tenuto	—	Well-articulated and full-length

Appendix 2

Glossary

Channel surfing: When watching TV, switching channels randomly as soon as you get tired of one channel or have seen enough to know what is going on at that channel. In music, it is kind of like switching music radio stations: as soon as you hear enough to know what is going on, you switch the channel. Some channels may attract you more than others, so you may listen to them longer.

Composer: A person who organizes and plans sounds and silence in a meaningful way.

Composing: Creating sounds in an organized way that is planned and prepared in advance; organizing sounds and silence in a creative and meaningful way.

Composition: Sounds that are organized by a person or a group of people in a purposefully planned way that can be repeated consistently.

Contrast: The concept of being noticeably different from something else. In music two or more differing ideas provide contrast and interest. Contrast can be achieved in many ways including changes in melody, rhythm, harmony, timbre, and range.

Form: The structure of a musical composition, such as ABA, sonata form, theme and variations, or rondo form (in other words, how a piece is organized).

Graphic notation: Notation for composition that uses visual imagery to represent sounds.

Harmony: A combination of two or more musical tones performed at the same time to produce chords.

    Major chord: Three notes with the intervals Major third plus minor third.
    Minor chord: Three notes with the intervals minor third plus major third.

Cluster chord: Two or more notes in a "cluster" such as Major second plus major second.

Improvising: Making up music on the spot without planning it out or writing it down.

Layering: Putting things on top of one another. In music, this involves putting musical ideas on top of one another, having them played at the same time.

Melody: A series of musical tones that are grouped together to make a single musical idea.

Music: Sound and silence organized through time that says something to the listener or has meaning to the listener.

Ostinato: A pattern of notes that is repeated many times and can be used to accompany other musical ideas. (Original Italian word meaning is stubborn, or persistent, as in the pattern is continually repeated and won't stop!)

Pattern: A regular or repetitive form or a repeated design.

Pentatonic scale: A five-note scale. (One common pentatonic scale uses these pitches from a major scale: 1, 2, 3, 5, 6.)

Range: How high and low an instrument can play.

Repose: Rest or calm; relaxed; temporary rest from excitement or activity.

Resolution (repose): When a musical phrase feels like it has come to an end; when a dissonance moves to a consonance; when a rhythm comes to a rest or a steady place.

Rhythm: A pattern of beats in music.

   Triple: A feeling or grouping of three beats.
   Duple: A feeling or grouping of two beats.

Scale: A set of notes that ascends and descends according to given rules.

   Major scale rule: Whole step, whole, half, whole, whole, whole, half.
   Pentatonic scale: Whole step, whole, minor third, whole.

Soundscape: A collection of sounds organized and put together. As a painter paints a landscape, the composer can create a soundscape.

Syllable: A part or whole of a word having one vowel sound.

Texture: How music can sound thick or thin and how complex it sounds rhythmically and harmonically:

Monophony: "One sound"; one melody line only; no accompaniment; can be more than one instrument or voice (thick) or a single instrument or voice (thin), as long as the same notes and rhythms are being played.

Homophony: One melody with chords accompanying (blended, like homogenized milk). Most popular music, such as rock, folk, and country music, uses homophony. In pure homophony, all voices move in the same rhythm.

Polyphony: "Many sounds"; two or more melodies, equally important, at the same time. (The melodies should have different rhythms.)

Tension: When there is rhythmic fighting, harmonic complexity (dissonance), melodic intensity.

Timbre: The quality of a sound that makes it unique from other sounds, such as the difference in quality between a trumpet sound and a violin sound performing the exact same pitch. Instrumentation and color are other simple ways to refer to timbre.

Traditional notation: Music notes with stems and heads on a five-line staff (traditional Western art music notation).

Unity: The concept of several similar ideas forming a complete and pleasing whole. A piece of music is unified when there are elements that tie it together, such as rhythm, melody, or harmony.

Variations: Modifying a melody or main musical theme so it has new, contrasting parts, yet is similar enough to be recognized as the main theme.

Word painting (text-painting): When a composer tries to represent a certain word or idea in a specific way with music. For example, for the word *sunrise*, the composer could choose to have rising musical lines, perhaps upward-moving scales, representing the sun rising up in the sky. To represent "anger," a composer might choose very loud, accented, dissonant chords.

Appendix 3

Sample Evaluation Form for Student Compositions

Appendix 3

Rubric: Sample quality line for grading student assignments—12 points total

Name: _____ Date: _____

Sample Rubric for Evaluating Compositions

	0–1 Point	2 Points	3 Points	4 Points
Aesthetic	Needs work; or no evidence of effort	One or more interesting ideas, but not effective musically; may come across as scattered or repetitive	Interesting musical ideas, and moderately effective; composition might benefit from more consistency or more diversity	Terrific! Strong aesthetic appeal and general impression; engages the listeners in an emotional and/or meaningful time
Creativity	No variety or exploration of elements of music such as rhythm and melody	Musical ideas are okay, but lack variety, or exploration of elements of music such as rhythm, timbre, texture, and melody	Involves some original aspects or manipulations of musical ideas; explores and varies two or more elements of music, such as rhythm, timbre, texture, and melody	Includes very original, unusual, or imaginative musical ideas; explores and varies multiple musical elements such as rhythm, timbre, texture, and melody
Craftsmanship	Gives no sense of a completed musical idea; meter and/or rhythm is inconsistent without reason	Presents at least one complete idea; meter and rhythm are mostly correct, but may have one or two places that seem like they don't fit; composition may lack a feeling of overall completeness; composition may feel disorganized and random	Ending feels final; good use of meter and rhythm; uses at least two musical elements to organize the musical ideas and overall form	Presents at least one complete musical idea; uses multiple elements of music to good effect and is organized well; includes tempo, articulations, dynamics, phrasing, and other important score markings

Additional comments:

Total points: ____

Total Points Table
   Total points: _____

Total points = letter grade as below:				
10–12 = A	7–9 = B	4–6 = C	1–3 = D	0 = F

Appendix 4
Creative Warm-Ups for Band

Creative conducting improvisations (great as a warm-up, or middle of the rehearsal tension releaser):

1. Explain that when conductors put their hands up HIGH, students should play "high" pitches and hands LOW equals low pitches. Pointing at individuals or specific groups or sections means those people should play. Typical visual cutoffs and entrances can be given as well as visual communication for pulsating notes, ostinatos, jabs, swells, decrescendos, and so on. The wave is especially fun!

2. SOLO time can happen where you point at one person and they make up a solo, or point to two people and have a duet, or trade off, pointing back and forth.

3. Usually, students are left to pick any notes in any key, with no concern for tonality. There are NO wrong notes. However, one advanced option can be to assign a specific key and have everyone stay diatonic in that key, or pentatonic, or another prescribed, limited note set.

4. Student conductors LOVE to participate AFTER the teacher has modeled some possibilities.

5. After the concept is understood, consider improvising specific pictures, feelings, or ideas, such as lesson 2 with the bird and the dog. The conductor/student leader may choose to share their "picture" or idea before or after they lead. Sharing it after allows the ensemble to try to think creatively in the music improvisation moments about what feelings or ideas the leader is trying to share visually and musically.

Appendix 5

Recommended Resources

BOOKS

Hickey, M. 1997. "Teaching Ensembles to Compose and Improvise." *Music Educators Journal* 83, no. 6: 17–21.

Hickey, M., ed. 2003. *Why and How to Teach Music Composition*. Reston, VA: MENC.

Hickey, M. 2012. *Music Outside the Lines: Ideas for Composing in K–12 Music Classrooms*. New York: Oxford University Press.

Hickey, M., A. Koops, C. Randles, D. A. Stringham, L. Thornton, and P. R. Webster. 2013. *Musicianship: Composing in Band and Orchestra*. Chicago: GIA.

Kaschub, M., and J. Smith. 2009. *Minds on Music: Composition for Creative and Critical Thinking*. Lanham, MD: Roman & Littlefield, in partnership with MENC.

Kerchner, J. L., K. Strand, and D. DiOrio. 2016. *Musicianship: Composing in Choir*. Chicago: GIA.

Koops, A. 2013. "Chapter 8: Facilitating Composition in Instrumental Settings." In *Composing Our Future: Preparing Music Educators to Teach Composition*, edited by M. Kaschub and J. Smith, 149–66. New York: Oxford University Press.

McLean, M. 2013. *Music Works: A Progressive Approach to Music Composition*. YCIW, Apple Books. iBooks (connects with Noteflight).

Riley, P. E. 2016. *Creating Music: What Children from Around the World Can Teach Us*. Lanham, MD: Rowman & Littlefield.

Ruthmann, A. 2007. "The Composers' Workshop: An Approach to Composing in the Classroom." *Music Educators Journal* 93, no. 4 (March): 38–43, www.jstor.org/stable/4127132.

WEBSITES

American Composers Forum Educational Resources. https://composersforum.org/education/educational-resources/.

American Composers Forum: BandQuest, ChoralQuest. Sample BandQuest curriculum: *Alligator Alley*, by Michael Daugherty (and other curriculum). https://composersforum.org/education/educational-resources/.

COMPOSER PAGES

Jodie Blackshaw. https://www.jodieblackshaw.com/.
Whirlwind (Free score download—Grade 1 band piece with soundscapes). Manhattan Beach Music. http://whirlwind.manhattanbeachmusic.com/html/score.html.

RECOMMENDED ONLINE COMPOSITION PROGRAMS

Noteflight. http://www.noteflight.com/.
Musescore. http://musescore.org/.
Flat. https://flat.io/.
Soundtrap. https://www.soundtrap.com.

COMPOSITION CONTESTS AND FESTIVALS

American Composers Forum NextNotes High School Composition Awards, apply at https://americancomposersforum.slideroom.com/.
National Association for Music Education (NAfME):
    Student Composers Competition: http://bit.ly/NAfMEStudentComposers.
    Electronic Music Competition: http://bit.ly/ElectronicMusicCompetition.
    Student Songwriters Competition: http://bit.ly/NAfMEStudentSongwriters.
Los Angeles Philharmonic Young Composer Awards. https://www.laphil.com/learn/learning-programs/national-composers-intensive/.

About the Authors

Dr. Alexander Koops is associate professor of music at Azusa Pacific University, director of the Azusa Conservatory Community Music School, Fulbright Scholar, and recipient of the California Music Educators Association (CMEA) John Swain Music Education Award. He regularly adjudicates and clinics middle school and high school bands and orchestras, leads composition workshops and professional development, and is a published author.

Dr. John L. Whitener is professor of music and coordinator of music education at California State University, Northridge, where he teaches music education courses in addition to teaching middle school band at Jordan Middle School, Burbank, California, and working as a professional composer. He has received numerous teaching awards including the Bravo Award given by the Los Angeles Music Center for Teaching Excellence in Music Education and the Outstanding Music Educator of the Year for CMEA, Southern California Division.

www.ingramcontent.com/pod-product-compliance
Lightning Source LLC
Chambersburg PA
CBHW070642300426
44111CB00013B/2217